T0382844

Self-Defense for Gentlemen and Ladies

Photograph signed "Col. Thos. H. Monstery," May 2, 1885. Courtesy of Hargrett Rare Book and Manuscript Library / University of Georgia Libraries.

SELF-DEFENSE
for Gentlemen *and* Ladies

A Nineteenth-Century Treatise on Boxing, Kicking,
Grappling, and Fencing with the Cane and Quarterstaff

Colonel Thomas Hoyer Monstery

Edited and Introduced by Ben Miller

BLUE SNAKE BOOKS
BERKELEY, CALIFORNIA

Published by Blue Snake Books,
an imprint of North Atlantic Books
Huichin, unceded Ohlone land
Berkeley, California

Cover photo of Thomas H. Monstery courtesy of Hargrett Rare Book and Manuscript Library / University of Georgia Libraries
Cover art by Bronwyn Frazier-Miller
Cover and book design by Brad Greene

Printed in the United States of America

Self-Defense for Gentlemen and Ladies: A Nineteenth-Century Treatise on Boxing, Kicking, Grappling, and Fencing with the Cane and Quarterstaff is sponsored and published by North Atlantic Books, an educational nonprofit based in the unceded Ohlone land Huichin (Berkeley, CA) that collaborates with partners to develop cross-cultural perspectives; nurture holistic views of art, science, the humanities, and healing; and seed personal and global transformation by publishing work on the relationship of body, spirit, and nature.

North Atlantic Books's publications are distributed to the US trade and internationally by Penguin Random House Publisher Services. For further information, visit our website at www.northatlanticbooks.com.

PLEASE NOTE: The creators and publishers of this book are not and will not be responsible, in any way whatsoever, for any improper use made by anyone of the information contained in this book. All use of the aforementioned information must be made in accordance with what is permitted by law, and any damage liable to be caused as a result thereof will be the exclusive responsibility of the user. In addition, they must adhere strictly to the safety rules contained in the book, both in training and in actual implementation of the information presented herein. This book is intended for use in conjunction with ongoing lessons and personal training with an authorized expert. It is not a substitute for formal training. It is the sole responsibility of every person planning to train in the techniques described in this book to consult a licensed physician in order to obtain complete medical information on their personal ability and limitations. The instructions and advice printed in this book are not in any way intended as a substitute for medical, mental, or emotional counseling with a licensed physician or health-care provider.

Library of Congress Cataloging-in-Publication Data
Monstery, Thomas Hoyer, 1824-1901.
   Self-Defense for gentlemen and ladies : a nineteenth-century treatise on boxing, kicking, grappling, and fencing with the cane and quarterstaff / Colonel Thomas Hoyer Monstery ; edited and introduced by Ben Miller.
      pages cm
   ISBN 978-1-58394-868-2 (Hard Cover) — ISBN 978-1-58394-869-9 (E-book)
   1. Self-defense. 2. Self-defense for women. 3. Martial arts weapons. 4. Martial arts—History—19th century. I. Miller, Ben, 1977- II. Title.
   GV1111.M58 2015
   613.6'6—dc23
                                                                                         2014035215

5 6 7 8 SHERIDAN 25 24 23

North Atlantic Books is committed to the protection of our environment. We print on recycled paper whenever possible and partner with printers who strive to use environmentally responsible practices.

Contents

Preface

I first learned of the great duelist and fencing master Thomas Hoyer Monstery several years ago, while researching ancient systems of European fencing and the various masters who taught them. That journey began in June of 2005, the day I first walked into the Martinez Academy of Arms in New York City.

I had been searching for a new martial art to begin training in, and the Academy was the fourth or fifth place on my list of schools to visit. Previously, I had studied Krav Maga and western boxing in New York, and Arnis stick fighting while living in the Philippines—all under notable instructors for whom I had great respect and admiration. And yet, I somehow felt unfulfilled in these martial arts. What, exactly, was missing, I did not know. But I was fairly certain that I would recognize it when I saw it.

I had never been interested in modern Olympic sport fencing, the purpose of which seemed to be about scoring points and winning at a game, rather than defending oneself in an actual combative situation. Whatever swordsmanship had been like hundreds of years ago, my reasoning and intuition told me that it little resembled what was now practiced on the Olympic strip. I had been told, however, that a different type of fencing was being practiced at the Martinez Academy in New York City—one with a martial mind-set. It seemed incumbent upon me to at least witness what was being practiced there.

What I found there was something far more extraordinary and significant: a surviving tradition of the older, martial styles of European swordsmanship—one of the last traditions in the world, in fact. Not only were the objective, mind-set, and form completely different, but the various systems taught at the Academy included a vast, almost countless number of techniques that had completely vanished from the modern sport. Additionally, the usage of ancient European weapons such as the rapier, sword and dagger, single dagger, cloak, staff, cane, military saber, and others were being taught. The Academy was run by Maestro Ramón Martínez and Maestro Jeannette Acosta-Martínez, the former having been taught these systems and techniques by his own master, *Maître d'Armes* Frederick Rohdes. A German born in 1897, and a veteran of at least one actual combat encounter with sharp broadswords, Rohdes had learned a variety of historical systems from his master, Marcel Cabijos, and others in Europe. Cabijos, a Frenchman and veteran of the First World War, had in 1926 notably defeated the épée and saber champion of the United States, Leo Nunes, with only a twelve-inch dagger.

In an age when Asian fighting systems had become synonymous with the term "martial arts," here was a rare, surviving vestige of Western heritage, a culturally fundamental art that had roots stretching back nearly a thousand years, and which I saw being executed with great control, finesse, speed, and precision. Whatever magic I had been looking for, I had found it at the Martinez Academy.

As I began training, I was surprised to learn that other fencing enthusiasts outside of the Academy, or at least those of my own generation, were completely unaware that any older, martial traditions had survived. This was understandable, considering that nearly all modern books and references on the subject of fencing said not a word about older surviving styles. These texts presumed either that the modern sport of fencing was no different than the fencing of past centuries, or that the older traditions had become utterly extinct. Maestro Martínez told me that Master Rohdes had assured him that the old systems, including the use of antiquated weapons, had endured in certain fencing schools scattered across Europe, having been passed down through the ages from master to student. If Rohdes was correct—and I had no reason to doubt that he was—then, I reasoned, some record of these masters and their techniques must have survived as well. The question I posed to myself was, could such evidence be found? If so, modern references would be of little or no use. It would be necessary to delve into rare, highly obscure period sources.

The quest to find such records led to more than six years of assiduous research—from libraries across the country, to old newspaper archives, to rare bookstores located in foreign countries. In the process of that research, I began to uncover a wealth of evidence attesting to the truth of what Rohdes had claimed—such traditions had indeed survived. Throughout recent centuries, a large number of masters—some famous, others obscure—continued to practice, preserve, and teach the old systems and techniques, even into the twentieth century.

And thus it was that I came across Thomas Hoyer Monstery, a Danish-American master who hailed from nineteenth-century New York, and, coincidentally, had operated a fencing academy on Bleecker Street, only six blocks from the one where I now trained. By all accounts, Monstery had led an amazing life. Not only was he a highly accomplished swordsman who had crossed blades with the greatest luminaries of his era, but his authority as a martial artist was bolstered by an incredible abundance of firsthand combative experiences. He had fought under twelve flags (on three separate continents), ascended to the rank of colonel, participated in more than fifty duels, and battled gangsters; he was constantly involved in the great conflicts and upheavals of his time. Despite these astounding feats, for years he was merely one of many masters that I continued to research, for the purpose of including in a larger work on the history of fencing.

That changed on October 6, 2010, when I stumbled upon what appeared to be an article on self-defense with the cane, authored by Monstery himself. The article's subtitle, "Chapter XIII," made it immediately clear to me that the piece was part of a larger series. With excitement, I sought out and obtained the remaining fragile chapters, all of which had been published in a nineteenth-century New York journal. After studying the work in its entirety, I realized that I had in my possession something of great significance. Here was Monstery's magnum opus, a highly detailed dissertation on the art and science of defense. Filled with profound insight, as well as shockingly practical advice based upon personal combative experience, Monstery's treatise propounded a holistic approach to self-defense, comprising both unarmed and armed methods, for use against a wide variety of fighting styles and weapons, and even went so far as to touch upon issues of health, exercise, diet, and longevity. Additionally, the treatise presented a unique glimpse into the Victorian fighting world, describing other styles of the era such as British "purring" (shin-kicking), Welsh jump-kicking, "scientific" Danish head-fighting, African American head-butting, and American rough-and-tumble fighting, the last of which involved biting and eye gouging. References to these styles elsewhere in the literature of the nineteenth century do exist, but they are few and far between, and Monstery's work appears to be the only one in existence that discusses how to defend against them in significant detail. Following the sections on boxing, kicking, and grappling, Monstery proceeds to the cane, an ideal weapon for street defense, which, he explains, is based on fencing principles similar to those of the broadsword or saber. Lastly, he concludes with a section on the quarterstaff, for practical use in the country or mountains. This segment is truly one of a kind, as it represents the only treatise on quarterstaff technique published in America prior to the twentieth century.

For their help in preparing this work for publication, I would like to thank the following people: my wife, Bronwyn Frazier-Miller, for her painstaking and time-consuming work redrawing Monstery's many illustrations, for restoring numerous photographs for the introduction and cover, and for her steadfast love and support; and Maestro Ramón Martínez and Maestro Jeannette Acosta-Martínez, for first encouraging me to publish this work, for their many years of mentorship on and off the *salle* floor, for their assistance with the glossary, and without whose invaluable guidance, advice, and counsel this book would not have been possible. Also, my parents David and Pam Miller, and Jack and Pam Frazier, for their generous support throughout the years; Jared Kirby, for giving me a copy of Frederick Whittaker's 1884 biography of Monstery, as well as for helping me acquire the rare nineteenth century Swedish texts which documented the fencing curriculum at Ling's Central Institute; Carl Massaro, for his insight into Monstery's wrestling, and help with the grappling terms in the glossary; Nigel Poulton, for his insight into Monstery's boxing material; Diane Hayes, the great-great-granddaughter of Colonel Monstery, who generously shared with me her articles, images, and knowledge about her distinguished ancestor; Erin Wiegand, my fantastic editor at North Atlantic Books; Michael Wen Sen Su, for his assistance with imaging; Joey Dembner, Brian Sechler, and Scott Hansen, for their feedback and advice; Susan Snyder, Head of Public Services at the Bancroft Library, University of California, Berkeley; Chuck

Barber, Assistant Director of the Hargrett Rare Book & Manuscript Library, University of Georgia; and William A. Mays, proprietor of the *National Police Gazette*, for allowing me to use numerous illustrations from the *Gazette* to supplement the introduction and chapter 11. Lastly, and most importantly, I am grateful to that force or spirit which guided me toward Monstery's articles on that fateful day.

After its initial run in the 1870s, Monstery's treatise disappeared into obscurity. One can only assume that its author must have been disappointed at the lack of distribution it received. In the opening pages of his work, he expressed the following wish:

> I desire to give the American people, among whom [my] life has been spent, the benefit of all the experience that I have acquired on the subject.

May it finally be so, and may Colonel Monstery's words be a beacon for those who seek to study, practice, preserve, and carry on the ancient traditions.

—Ben Miller
January 2015

PART ONE

Colonel Thomas Hoyer Monstery:
The Unknown American Martial Arts Master

During the winter of 1881, a reporter for the *New York Sun* paid a visit to a unique "School of Arms" located on Manhattan's Sixth Avenue. Later, he set down a description of this academy, and of the extraordinary individual who greeted him there:

> Specimens of old armor hung on the walls, flanked by curious and rare weapons, daggers, pikes, halberds, muskets, foils, rapiers, broadswords, plastrons, bracers, masks, boxing-gloves, Indian clubs, and dumbbells. The Colonel, tall, erect, martial, his coat buttoned closely around his slim form, a silk skull-cap set jauntily upon his brown locks, which were parted with military precision down the back of his head and brought forward over his ears, and his iron-gray mustache and goatee carefully waxed, seemed fittingly framed by the weapons around him.[1]

The man was Thomas Hoyer Monstery. He was a fencing master, boxer, marksman, sailor, adventurer, street fighter, soldier of fortune, animal tamer, and world traveler. He was a veteran of numerous wars, and an expert duelist, having participated in, by varying accounts, somewhere between fifty-two and sixty-one personal combats, and had twenty-two scars on his body to prove it. He was one of at least a dozen or so fencing masters in America still teaching the use of ancient European weapons such as the rapier, dagger, and

Colonel Thomas Hoyer Monstery.

quarterstaff, in addition to weapons still used on the battlefield such as the broadsword, knife, bayonet, pike, and lance. Also, unlike most fencing masters of his caliber and of his period, he was an American, or at least considered himself as such, though he could never quite shake the slight foreign accent acquired from the years spent abroad during his youth. He was, in his own words, a "Gothic American."[2]

CHILDHOOD AND EARLY TRAINING

Although it is impossible to distill the entire life of a man—especially one as varied and extraordinary as Monstery's—down to only a few pages, an overview of his life is merited.

Our subject was born Thomas Hoyer Mönster, on April 21, 1824, in Copenhagen, Denmark.[3] His father, an aristocrat of Irish ancestry, had been banished from the court of Denmark for slaying a man in a duel. He eventually died from the effects of a sword wound in the lungs when his son was a child. Monstery's only memory of his father was of the latter "standing erect in a nightshirt, stained with blood at the breast and a sword in his hand."[4]

The boy's martial training commenced at the age of twelve, when his family procured for him a place as a cadet in the Danish navy. There he endured a near-constant stream of abuse and the occasional brawl, forcing the young recruit to learn how to defend himself with his fists. During this time he also stabbed his first man in a fight, while on shore leave in Rio de Janeiro, Brazil.

At age seventeen, while serving aboard the ship *Bellona*, Monstery was injured by an accidental powder explosion, which rendered him temporarily blind and forever deprived him of the keen eyesight required for navigation and other tasks in the navy. Monstery was promptly discharged from the service and sent home. After lengthy medical attention, he regained his vision, although it was still severely impaired.

The boy was not yet deterred from pursuing a martial life. After recuperating, he enrolled in the Royal Military Institute of Gymnastics and Arms in Copenhagen, one of the leading European institutions of its kind. It was here that Monstery began his fencing career under the direction of Franz Nachtegall[5], and where he learned to handle "sword, musket, bayonet, rapier, cudgel and quarterstaff" with great proficiency. Although he was still nearly half-blind from the accident, and was forced to wear thick, powerful lenses, Monstery overcame his handicap while fencing by learning to rely on "feeling and the motion of his adversary." He graduated at the head of his class, listed as "Number One" in athletics of every kind, and was granted the rank of instructor at the military academy.[6]

Still desiring to become "the best swordsman in the world," Monstery traveled throughout Europe, seeking instruction from the best masters he could find. His journey brought him to Stockholm, Sweden, where he entered the Central Institute of Physical Culture, founded by the celebrated Dr. Pehr Henrik Ling. At the institute, Monstery learned a "brilliant and effective style of sword-play" that he would forever term the Swedish system, but which was, in fact, a modified version of the French style that Ling had learned from his own masters.[7] Notably, the fencing program at the institute specialized in ambidexterity (a skill which would later save Monstery's life), and provided instruction in unconventional weapons such as the rapier, dagger, single and double-handed axe, spear, and pike, even going so far as to train its adepts in how to fence with the dagger

Fencers using "unequal opposing weapons . . . in which the bayonet is opposed to the sabre," at Pehr Henrik Ling's Central Institute of Physical Culture, where Monstery trained during the 1840s.

versus the bayonet.[8] After four years of assiduous training, Monstery graduated from the Central Institute a Master of Arms.[9]

Monstery still felt that his martial education was incomplete. He was a master of the sword, but he also desired to be a master of unarmed methods of self-defense. Prior to coming to Stockholm, he had traveled the British Isles—reputed at that time to have the best boxers in all of Europe—where he took lessons from the famous boxing champion William Thompson, popularly known as "Bendigo." Here he had been disappointed. In Thompson, Monstery found a highly skilled fighter, but a bad teacher who had "no idea" about how to transmit his art to others. Monstery's lessons with the champion consisted of sparring sessions during which he was offered "the privilege of getting a licking as often as he wanted, at a guinea—or five dollars—a licking." Monstery still felt that something in his martial arts was missing.

While in Stockholm, Monstery heard rumor of a very great boxing master named Liedersdorff, a German of medium size and modest strength, reputed to be "the most wonderful fighter in the world." After his graduation from the Central Institute, Monstery traveled to Hamburg, where he sought out this obscure master and became his disciple. Monstery's biography recounts:

> In Liedersdorff...he found a quiet, gentlemanly person, who looked more like a clergyman than a pugilist; and when he asked for lessons he was told to put on the gloves and try to hit his teacher, who promised not to hit him in return. This was quite a change from the Bendigo system, which consisted of knocking the pupil down as often as he could stand it, at a guinea a lesson.
>
> Monstery thought it would be fun, so he dashed at Liedersdorff, Bendigo style, and found himself turned round in a moment, stumbling about like a fool, not only unable to hit his teacher, but even to keep his face to him, for he was sent spinning round like a top and felt that he was completely at the mercy of this quiet-looking Liedersdorff, had the latter chosen to hit him.
>
> Here was something new of which Bendigo had no idea, and the young man set to work to learn it, and soon found that with it he could initiate quite a new science of sparring, devoid of brutality and eminently useful.[10]

Now thoroughly schooled in the ways of the fist, Monstery traveled to Southern Europe, which he had heard was home to the greatest knife fighters in the world. After traveling throughout Spain and

Italy, and taking part in numerous contests of arms, Monstery was surprised to discover that he had nothing left to learn. As his biographer noted, "He could beat them all, even at the knife play, by the secret he had learned at Stockholm, which he describes in three words: *Economy of motions.*"

After beating numerous Spanish and Italian fencers, Monstery set his sights on Paris, where he trounced the renowned French fencing master, Augustin Grisier, disarming him twice in a public assault. He could now hold his own with some of the best masters in Europe. He was still in his early twenties.

CAREER AS A DUELIST AND ADVENTURER

From there, Monstery traveled the world—to Vienna, Berlin, and St. Petersburg, where he was made chief fencing instructor in the Russian army, and the commanding officer of the Grand Duke

Constantine's bodyguard, eventually attaining the rank of colonel. North America and South America were next. There he fought as a soldier of fortune in innumerable wars and conflicts. If the figures published during his lifetime are to be believed, he served under the flags of twelve different countries: Denmark, Russia, the United States, Nicaragua, Cuba (during the Cuban insurrection with General Lopez), Colombia, Spain, Honduras, San Salvador, Costa Rica, Guatemala, and Mexico.[11] Although there is not nearly enough space here to recount his many combats and adventures (and, in fact, a book containing those has already been written[12]), a few incidents are worth mentioning, as they serve as a testament to the Colonel's incredible prowess and experience as a martial artist.

In 1858, while taking part in an ill-fated expedition to Honduras, Monstery was arrested on suspicion of being a revolutionary. One day, while strolling about the prison courtyard, he passed too close to one of the soldiers on guard. Mistakenly believing that Monstery was trying to escape, the guard attempted to bayonet him. Years later, in an interview, the aging Colonel described what happened next:

> I had no idea of escape, but was forced to defend myself. I took his musket from him and stunned him with my fist. At that moment eight others, armed with muskets and bayonets, sprang out of the guardhouse and attacked me. Then followed one of the fights of my life. I demonstrated there that Dumas's back-to-the-wall heroes were frauds. I would have been stuck like a pig but for the fact that I had a space in which to maneuver. They knew nothing, of course, of scientific bayonet play, and their weapons fortunately were unloaded. I had pinked two of them, broken the bayonets of three, and was nearly fainting from exhaustion when I heard a stern command behind me: "Halt!" My opponents dropped their weapons. Turning I

saw [Commandant] Valdarama, who was standing in the doorway, an interested spectator of the bout from its beginning. He approached me and looked me over. "My God," he said. "Can a man learn to do that?" I told him that a sure-enough man could. He gave me my liberty at once and in return I gave him instruction.[13]

And so, at thirty-four years of age, Monstery went from being a prisoner to a combat instructor in the blink of an eye.

While serving in South America, Monstery never ceased testing his skills against other fighters. He engaged in numerous contests of arms against local fencing masters and *spadachins* (sword-wielding bravos); he even participated in bullfights. At one point, he was captured by indigenous rebels and tied to a tree for torture. Monstery escaped his bonds, sprinted three hundred yards through a hail of gunfire, plunged into a stream, and was swept over a waterfall.

Monstery's fencing skills also saved his life on the battlefield numerous times. During a battle in Chiapas, Mexico, while commanding a local cavalry troop, he was cut off from his main force of men, and quickly found himself surrounded on all sides. A contemporary article recounted how

he emptied three saddles with his revolvers before they closed in on him, and a fourth man fell before a thrust of his lance. The attacking party threw themselves from their horses, and one of them stabbed his horse in the chest, piercing its heart. The animal fell, pinning its rider under it, and for a moment he lay at the mercy of his enemies. In five seconds twenty blows fell on him. He was freed by the death struggles of his steed and hobbled to his feet. His left knee had been broken by the fall, and he stood on one leg like a stork. His lance, too, had been smashed, but he still held to the business end of it. As one of the white cross men turned to flee, Monstery leveled this broken bit of lance like a javelin and sent it through him at a distance of five yards, with such force that the spear-head projected a foot beyond the breast. The man fell upon his face, gasping. Balancing himself on one foot and partly braced by the dead body of his horse, against which he leaned, the master of arms drew the rapier, which had never failed him, and engaged his five adversaries. The young officer was first to fall before a [thrust] that caught him on the throat. A trooper who sprang in with clubbed musket was struck with such violence that the hilt thumped against his breast bone. As he fell the sword snapped. The other three leaped back out of reach of the terrible American and began reloading their muskets, intending to finish him at leisure. At this juncture some of Monstery's victorious riders broke from the chaparral in pursuit of stragglers, and his assailants fled.[14]

During his time abroad in Europe and the Americas, Monstery was involved in a vast number of duels. As to the exact number, the sources differ. His biography states that he participated in nineteen "regular duels" with the small-sword, plus forty-two with the saber, knife, and pistol.[15] The *New York Sun* states that he took part in fifty-three, and of these, served as principal in twenty-three.[16] The *Daily Globe* put the total at fifty-two.[17] Whatever the actual number, even the most conservative estimates are extraordinary, and put him in the same league as the most accomplished American duelists.

At least several detailed accounts of Monstery's duels survive. Of these, perhaps the most interesting is that which describes his encounter with the Mexican General Bragamonte. This account is notable for mentioning specific fencing techniques involving seizures and disarms with the left hand:

> [Bragamonte] sprung forward like a tiger, cutting high and low with
> all his force, and shouting savagely at every cut, while the American

stood cool at every turn. Bragamonte even cut at the ground, and one vicious slash grazed Monstery's foot, cut through the boot, and slightly wounded his great toe, though he did not feel it at the time. But at last Bragamonte wearied, and [Monstery] became the assailant in turn, cutting lightly and cautiously and always on guard.

At length Bragamonte tried his last secret trick, which would have puzzled any merely school fencer. Monstery made a light cut at his arm, outside, and Bragamonte threw up his own sword to bind his enemy's blade there, quick as a flash threw forward his left foot and clutched for Monstery's sword-wrist with his left hand.

It was the end of the duel.

Quicker than even the Spaniard, the American threw forward his own left foot, drawing back his sword out of danger, and in an instant had reversed the trick.

Bragamonte's sword-wrist was in his grasp, and he plunged his own blade deep into the Spaniard's vitals, so that the point came out behind Bragamonte's back, and the hilt struck his breast.[18]

Despite receiving this serious wound, Bragamonte survived, although, according to Monstery, he never "shone" as a swordsman again.

Monstery entered into duels for numerous reasons. His first had been fought over the affections of a woman; others were in response to personal injuries or insults to his own reputation. Monstery was an ardent nationalist, and more than once took up a blade or pistol to defend the honor of his adopted homeland. One such combat occurred in Mexico City, when an army colonel "made public reflections upon America and Americans, and [Monstery] resented it with a blow." They fought with pistols, and Monstery shattered the Mexican's arm at the shoulder.[19] Another time, during the height of the American Civil War in 1863, he was having dinner with friends when a member of the company, an expert fencer named Victor La Lieux, cast severe aspersions upon the character of the Union Army.

Wine glasses were overturned, chairs upset, and in a trice Col. Monstery had the speaker by the throat. A patriot like the colonel, who had fought for liberty in Sweden, Poland and Hungary could not brook the taunting insult to the flag of freedom in America and his passion got the better of his judgment. La Lieux and Monstery both being noted duelists, a challenge followed as a matter of course.

*The earliest known likeness of Monstery (seen at top center), about thirty-nine or forty years of age, sketched circa 1864. From Edward Jump's **San Francisco at the Fair,** 1864.* Courtesy of the Bancroft Library, University of California, Berkeley.

The combat was fought the next morning, with swords. At the outset of the duel, Monstery received a disabling wound in his sword arm. This might have been the end for many duelists, but Monstery simply switched his weapon to his left hand, having trained to fence with both. Although the duel was intended to end in death, it terminated when the Colonel "made a thrust at the same time that he parried a blow."[20] La Lieux was struck in his glass eye, which sprang from its socket and rolled upon the grass. The combat was halted. The two forgave each other, and dined together that evening on "all the terrapin and champagne that Baltimore afforded."[21]

Monstery's nationalistic feeling was often directed against the French, who had treated him with contempt during his stay in Paris, and had dismissed his victories there as "merely a case of a young man with a strong wrist" whose fencing style "was not fencing at all."[22] Many years later, when an editor for the *Chicago Tribune* was challenged to a duel by a bellicose French marquis, Monstery publicly volunteered to fight in the editor's stead. His offer noted:

> I will fight him for the honor of America against France with any of the following weapons, he of course, being entitled to choose the weapons:
>
> Pistols at ninety feet, advance and fire at will.
>
> Épée combat (triangular swords).
>
> Sabers or any cutting swords; cuts alone, no thrusts.
>
> Bayonets, as you please.
>
> Bowie knifes, and "no protection" if he desires to renew his experience in the wild West.
>
> With the fist, go as you please, no time.

Monstery qualified this offer with his preference that the marquis not choose firearms, explaining:

I prefer a shiny weapon. I am of a kind, philanthropic disposition, and as firearms demand, even with the most skillful shot, to aim at the heart, allowing for misses, a man is a murderer at the beginning. Humanity may not then be displayed. On the contrary, with the shiny weapon I would only attempt to clip the wings of my honored opponent. Should my philanthropic remarks be misconstrued, state that if my honored opponent wants death he can find it.[23]

While these excerpts, taken out of context, might suggest a hot-tempered or belligerent disposition, it should be noted that Monstery was nearly always described by those who knew him as courteous, affable, and charitable.[24] Further insight into Monstery's views on dueling can be gleaned from his biography, which explains his philosophy as follows:

. . . he strongly disapproves of it in a civilized State, yet he holds that there may be times when a duel is necessary as redress for an injury for which the law does not give any redress, while the opinion of society calls a man a coward if he suffers it tamely. In such a case it is the object of the "code of honor," so called, to provide for a contest that will not endanger life, except in aggravated cases, and until society provides a remedy for these injuries, dueling will always exist in some form or another, no matter how many laws are passed against it.[25]

Despite Monstery's large number of duels, he mentioned only two that resulted in the deaths of his opponents—his first, fought at age twenty-one, and another fought in Mexico in 1868.[26] In his capacity as a second and advisor, Monstery also claimed that he had "prevented more than fifty [duels] at different times of his life."[27]

Career as a Fencing Master

In later years, Monstery's personality seems to have mellowed somewhat, as he all but ceased fighting duels, and instead devoted his energies to teaching and mentoring others. He opened his first fencing and boxing academy in Baltimore, in 1851, where he trained a group of young men to defend against the Plug Uglies, at that time one of the most violent and notorious gangs in America. Monstery himself was threatened and attacked on several occasions by members of the gang, and was forced to protect himself with his fists, guns, and various improvised weapons.[28]

After serving abroad as a soldier of fortune, he returned to the United States in 1861 and began teaching on a near-permanent basis, opening several *salle d'armes* across the country—in San Francisco, Oakland, New York, and Chicago.[29] During this time he engaged in public contests and exhibitions with some of the most notable masters of the fencing world, such as Agesilao Greco, Carlo Pessina, and Eugenio Pini. Monstery often held his own against them, as reported in newspapers of the era:

> To conclude, Chev. Pini and Col. Monstery. The last [contest] was one of the most interesting events of the evening. Col. Monstery, with Pini, showed wonderful address and agility. No formal score was taken, but the Colonel made seven hits to four.[30]

Monstery also participated in a highly controversial contest with the French master Regis Senac, with whom he would engage in a long-standing feud.[31] Their assault took place in 1876, at Tammany Hall on Fourteenth Street, and encompassed the following weapons:

Foil.	12 points
Sabre	9 points
Rapier (cut and thrust)	12 points
Bayonet (thrust).	9 points
Knife (cut and thrust)	9 points[32]

The accounts of this contest differ considerably—the *New York Times* claimed that the presiding judge was biased toward Monstery, while a more detailed account published in the *Army and Navy Journal* claimed that the judge was partial to Senac, and that Monstery actually won twenty-one of the twenty-seven points awarded. Witnesses described how, instead of deciding disputed hits, the "incompetent" referee "argued with the inflamed seconds and appealed to the audience," and later "shrugged his shoulders and looked the picture of irresolution."[33] Taken together, the various reports seem to suggest that Senac bested Monstery with the foil, while the Colonel surpassed the Frenchman with the saber and rapier. The entire contest came to an end when, prior to the conclusion of the rapier assault, Monstery walked off of the stage in disgust, and "the whole affair broke up in disorder."[34] Although the Frenchman was officially adjudged the winner, Senac himself seemed to acknowledge the inconclusiveness of the contest, when four years later he challenged Monstery to yet again "fight a match with him . . . for the championship of America"—a challenge that Monstery apparently ignored.[35]

Whatever the true magnitude of Monstery's skill, if judged by the success of his students, he must have been an extraordinary teacher. One of his pupils, the actor Francis Wilson, recounted how Monstery's careful training enabled him to win the amateur fencing championship of America in 1878.[36] While still a young man, Wilson sought out Monstery to learn pugilism for the purposes of defending

Portrait of Monstery with broadsword.

himself against the abuses of a bullying roommate; after the Colonel's instruction proved fruitful in this regard, Wilson went to live with Monstery at his New York academy, where the two of them would "have numerous bouts at unheard-of hours of the night."[37] The qualities imparted by Wilson's mentor were well described in a detailed account of the contest, which was held at Gilmore's Garden before an "immense" crowd:

> [Mr. Sernmig] opened the assault with Wilson, a pupil of Colonel Monstery, and one whose style on guard is perfect and graceful, the body covered, but not crouching too low, prepared for advance or retreat. It was soon plain that Wilson had the sympathy of the audience, who applauded him warmly as he rapidly counted five hits to his opponent's two, and became an easy victor. It was noticeable that Wilson, besides being the better fencer, was the most polite. All the points he made he had to claim, while he courteously saluted the hits of his opponent, a matter of good breeding in which the other fencers of the entertainment were deficient, but which cannot be too much commended in a public assault.[38]

The contest took a dramatic turn when the two finalists were announced. Wilson was to fence G. C. Barnett, a student of Regis Senac, and an "old swordsman" whose "crouching" guard position was described as "something like an Indian in a knife fight." Earlier, between bouts, Barnett had attempted to intimidate Wilson by "recounting the number of people he had slain in the mimic contest in Cuba and Spain and France."[39] The account continued,

> The two victors then advanced to decide the championship, Barnett and Wilson, the one all grace, the other silent but dangerous to look at. A rattling bout was now expected, Barnett having the experience to back him. To the surprise of the whole house, however,

Barnett had no chance from the first. Wilson had been watching his game, and what was more important, Wilson's second, none other than Col. Monstery, had been watching it too. The youngster—for Wilson is a mere boy—obeyed orders, kept out of distance, would not engage with the *glizade*, but gave a rapid beat on the blade, and a straight lunge in low carte, and the dangerous Barnett was hit. Four times he played the same game, and each time got home, the count standing three to nothing, one hit being ruled out as a scratch. Considering that young Wilson had not fenced for two years, till he took twenty-four lessons of Col. Monstery, the result was a great triumph for the Colonel and his pupil, who was hailed with cheers as the Amateur Fencing Champion of America.[40]

Soon after this contest, Wilson invited several of his fellow fencers to Monstery's school, where he arranged for them to view an assault between himself and his teacher. Wilson recounted, "With the confidence born of victory I made up my mind to give Monstery the toughest bout of his existence if I had to break my neck in the effort."[41] Momentarily catching the Colonel off guard, Wilson succeeded in disarming him. But this was not the end of the exchange. Wilson described what happened next:

> When I tried to follow up the advantage, he deftly disarmed me with his bare hand and turned the point of my sword against me.

Years later, after Wilson achieved great fame as an actor, he wrote in his memoirs that Monstery was "probably the most expert swordsman who ever made America his home," and noted that "even now, when I go to Chicago, where he resides, my old master and I have many an enjoyable bout with the foils."[42]

Monstery also trained two of America's most renowned theatrical actors—Junius Brutus Booth, and his brother Edwin Booth—though not the youngest and most notorious member of the family, John Wilkes Booth. Wilson recounted how he and Junius, together, had visited their old preceptor—"the bewaxed moustached Colonel"— and discussed their acting ambitions as well as fencing.[43] In 1881, Monstery explained how he came to train Junius, who would go on to become one of the stage's most accomplished swordsmen:

> He came to me to learn to fence just because he had been badly injured in fencing on the stage. Once he got a bad cut on the forehead. You see his opponent forgot his cuts, the 'one, two, three' business, and so when Booth cut down, as he should have done, the man cut him over the head. At another time he was badly cut in the knee, much in the same way. So he came to me to learn the art of fencing in pure self-defense. And what a superb swordsman he became![44]

Monstery also mentored one of the greatest swordswomen of the nineteenth century—Ella Hattan, popularly known as "Jaguarina." When she was eighteen, Hattan became a pupil of Monstery at his New York school. According to the *New York Times*,

> The Colonel declared he would make the little girl the greatest woman fencer of her time, and from him she learned all she knew of the art.[45]

Actually, she had begun training at eight years of age, having first learned to fence with the foil and knife from her mother, a Spaniard. Still, it was from Monstery that Hattan acquired proficiency with the saber and broadsword—the weapons she would use to win the vast majority of her contests. After training for three years under the Colonel, she left to travel the world, and became a sensation with the foil, saber, broadsword, singlestick, rapier, dagger, bayonet, lance,

Spanish knife, and bowie knife, defeating fencing heavyweights such as Sergeant Owen Davis of the U.S. Cavalry, the famed knife duelist Charles Engelbrecht of the Danish Royal Guard, and the fencing master E. N. Jennings of the Royal Irish Hussars.[46] In 1884, after Monstery had moved his School of Arms to Chicago, Hattan reunited with her old mentor for a lively public fencing contest. In the resulting encounter between the two, one master and the other student, it was recorded that

> In the encounter with Monstery, at the end of a four hours' bout neither of the parties had gained a point, and the combat was declared a draw.[47]

By 1897, Hattan had defeated sixty men in contests on foot as well as on horseback, and was declared "the only woman in the world who has...been able to wrest championship honors from men of the greatest skill in the use of all chivalric weapons." For the past twelve years, asserted the *Boston Daily Globe*, she had "met all comers in mounted contests, and has never been defeated in a battle for general points."[48] Of these opponents, twenty-seven were said to have been masters-at-arms—a statistic verified by at least one major newspaper.[49] As a result of these combats, Hattan carried scars on her face, arms, and body.[50] Still, more than one male reporter, expecting to meet a "fierce faced Amazon," was shocked to find that Hattan exuded grace, refinement, and, as one put it, "perfect self-control and sweetness."[51] As Hattan herself explained,

> I'm a firm believer in the philosophy that women were meant to be just as robust and hardy as men—and they can be without losing any of their womanliness. In fact, physical culture gives grace, beauty, self-reliance—while taking nothing but aches and dyspepsia.[52]

In addition to her prowess at arms, Hattan also evinced a profound intellect and eloquence, especially in her statements regarding health and physical culture:

> If the people of the world were, all at once, transformed into original beings, as intended by nature, there would be little left to do for doctors and instructors in physical development. The so-called advancements in civilization have obliterated our natural selves to such a degree that the first requisites of nature to a healthful condition of the body are so obscured that by the time a man or woman of the present has fairly entered upon life they are so artificial, so unreal in their existence that they require teaching how to live. The whole secret of good health, and a fair physical development, is in returning to the first principles of nature . . . The very simplicity of the thing constitutes its chief mystery. It is only because we have outlived all plainness and all that is simple and natural that we are forced to resort to complicated expedients to undo the evils resulting from unnatural and artificial living.[53]

In comparing such statements to Monstery's own writings, it is almost impossible not to notice the influence of Hattan's old mentor, whose maxim was "follow nature in your living." For, although Hattan gave credit to various other fencing teachers (such as an "old actor," and a Mexican cavalry officer), it is telling that in all of her interviews, Monstery is the only instructor she ever mentioned by name—and repeatedly. In 1898, she stated simply that "Colonel Monstery of Chicago, a famous old Danish swordsman who had fought in the Mexican war, was my teacher."[54] Later, in a 1903 interview,

*Opposite: Monstery's most accomplished student, Ella Hattan,
popularly known as "Jaguarina."* Image courtesy of William A.
Mays, proprietor of the National Police Gazette.

Hattan's advice on how to attain proficiency in fencing can be seen as a partial tribute to Monstery: "My advice to people who wish to learn to fence is to go to a good master."[55]

Monstery was unusual in that he encouraged women to take up fencing long before it was both popular and fashionable for them to do so.[56] As early as 1881, he stated that

> [Fencing] makes a woman active—quick to see; gives her command of her limbs, enables her to protect herself in the street, to move quickly and with certainty... It brings the color to her cheek, elasticity to her limbs, and adds years to her life.[57]

And again, in a later interview:

> Ladies as fencers are superior to gentlemen in many respects. They surpass the male pupils in quickness, in determination, and the peculiar kind of endurance and nerve-forces required.[58]

By all accounts, Monstery's instruction was highly formalized and rigorous. According to one observer, he "preserved his military air under all circumstances, even toward his charming pupils."[59] Regarding her own training, Hattan recalled that Monstery "knew her ability, but was determined that she should learn confidence by experience and hard knocks."[60] In 1891, a journalist visiting Monstery's school gave a brief account of the training that the Colonel put his female students through:

> Though she looked as if she couldn't harm a fly, Miss Marsh stood her ground admirably, and her flexible wrist instantly responded to every thrust made at her face, chest, arms and hands... The veteran

Opposite: Photograph of Ella Hattan, popularly known as "Jaguarina," published in 1906. Image courtesy of National Police Gazette Enterprises, LLC.

professor, ancient Col. Monstery, stood by in close proximity, with foil raised on high, ready to check the excessive ardor of these charming champions. And as the ribbons of steel clashed, joined and sundered, the old veteran called out:

"Tie!"

"Charge!"

"Disengage!"

"Coupez!"

"Now a counter tierce!"

"Excellent septime!"

"Battez mains!"

And so the hints and the instructive phrases fell from his lips with lightning speed, but often not quite enough to save this or that one of his pupils from a thrust.[61]

Monstery claimed that he taught his female pupils no differently than he did men.[62] Nor was his instruction limited to the art of the sword; in 1888, he was also teaching "two classes of lady-boxers."[63] Additionally, Monstery included a special drill in his curriculum intended to prepare his female pupils for potential street encounters:

After a lady becomes reasonably expert with the foils, the Colonel puts his fair pupil through an exercise with a parasol, teaching her how to use it as a weapon of defense. The natural feminine impulse in a case of emergency, demanding the use of a weapon, would be to strike with it as with a club—a blow that would excite the derision of the person attacked. He teaches as a substitute a sort of bayonet thrust, which would break a rib, or a one-handed thrust, that would put out an eye.[64]

Perhaps due to this level of encouragement, Monstery was able to attract a remarkable number of high-profile female students, securing the tuition of actresses such as Mildred Holland, Lola Montez, Helen Temple, Ada Isaacs Menken, Adele Belganie, Maude Forrester, Helen King, Marie Jansen, Alice Trudell, and Pauline Kelly.[65] Under Monstery's guidance, Holland, according to one account, became "one of the most expert fencers in America."[66] By contrast, Regis Senac, when interviewed during the same period, noted that he did have young women pupils, "but not many."[67] Monstery also claimed to be one of the first masters of the period to hold public exhibitions featuring female fencers. After the Austrian master Johann Hartl and his troupe of Viennese female fencers demonstrated sword and dagger technique in Chicago,[68] Monstery remarked that

> The Viennese lady fencers were not the first to exhibit their art in Chicago. In 1886 the ladies of the conservatory gave an exhibition in the Chicago Opera House. In fact, I believe we originated the idea.[69]

One can only wonder if Monstery was somehow instrumental in fostering the female fencing trend which exploded in the late 1890s.

Image from the 1886 article "Maids of Muscle," purporting to show Monstery teaching self-defense to a female student. From Weekly Inter Ocean, November 30, 1886.

THE USE OF ANCIENT WEAPONS

Monstery was also one of a select number of fencing masters in the United States teaching the use of antiquated weapons such as the rapier, dagger, and quarterstaff. As early as 1861, he was offering instruction at his academy in dagger, lance, "and other offensive and defensive arts."[70] Two years later, the following account of a fencing exhibition appeared in the pages of a major San Francisco newspaper:

> The Professor of Arms of the Club, Colonel T. H. Monstery... gave an exhibition of the use of the sword and dagger, with the aid of three of his pupils, Messrs. Mel, Johnson and McComb. The bout was opened with a simulated duel with foils, by Mel and Johnson,— Colonel Monstery and Mr. McComb acting as seconds. Two thrusts each were recorded, and then the seconds engaged with the same weapons; the Colonel thrust his adversary twice, and allowed him to make one in return. Then Mel and Johnson were respectively challenged by the Professor to attack him with broadswords, while the dagger only was used to defend, and all the blows were successfully parried by the Colonel with his apparently insignificant weapon.[71]

The next year, in 1864, Mark Twain was in the audience during a similar exhibition, after which he remarked, "The broadsword exercises by Col. Monstery and his pupils were among the most interesting features of the entertainment, and the dagger fencing, and dagger against broadsword were savagely delightful... The rapier fencing, between Col. Monstery and a pupil, was exquisitely graceful and beautiful."[72]

During the 1870s, Monstery engaged in at least three major public contests with the rapier, a thrust-and-cut weapon often used in conjunction with a dagger, with roots stretching back to the Renaissance.[73] Although the rapier had been largely eclipsed by the lighter smallsword around 1715, it still continued to hold sway in various places in Europe—especially Spain and Southern Italy, where it was used in duels.[74] During the nineteenth century, the French *épée de combat*, a lighter, thrust-only weapon, was often erroneously referred to as a "rapier" in English language publications, a fact which can make it difficult for the modern reader to discern exactly which weapon is being referred to in nineteenth century sources. Evidence indicates, however, that Monstery was using an actual rapier. Firsthand accounts of his famous contest with Regis Senac describes how the two used a "rapier," described as a "straight sword" with a "buttoned blade" with which they employed both "cuts and thrusts."[75] In a French language challenge to Monstery, Senac himself referred to the weapon used as a "rapière" rather than as an *épée de combat*.[76] And later, in 1880, Monstery was challenged by the Cuban fencing master José Recio Betancourt, with the stipulation that "instead of the sabre we might fence with the rapier, cut and thrust."[77] Senac also fought similar rapier contests with other fencing masters of the period, in which it was noted that "striking with both sides" of the blade was allowed (the blade of a true rapier being double-edged).[78]

Evidence suggests that Monstery's rapier and dagger technique did not die with him, but was transmitted to his students. In 1895, a fencing exhibition and lecture on self-defense at the Women's League in New York featured a "rapier and dagger bout" between Miss Olive Oliver and Pauline Willard. The presiding Chairman of the Fencing Committee, it was noted, was none other than Mildred Holland, Monstery's star female pupil from nearly fifteen years earlier.[79]

In 1876, another interesting fencing exhibition was announced, to be held at the Lyceum Theater under Monstery's direction, that

Col. T. H. MONSTERY'S
NEW YORK
Salle d'Armes,
619 SIXTH AVE., N. Y.

Fencing, Boxing and Shooting taught thoroughly and by approved methods.

Gentlemen desiring to practice will find ample room and every convenience, including baths, etc.

TERMS OF MEMBERSHIP:
Use of the establishment, $40 per annum ; $25 for six months ; $5 per month.

1874 advertisement for Monstery's New York Academy.

would involve "all kinds of weapons that are used in fencing." It was noted that the contestants would include Danes, Germans, Spaniards, Frenchmen, Englishmen, and Americans, and that the weapons used "would embrace the Spanish knife, the French quarterstaff, the English single stick, the German schlager," as well as the Bowie knife, cane, sword-cane, lance, bayonet, English quarterstaff, and "all kinds of swords, and with each the method of using it in actual combat will be shown."[80]

Judging by the various descriptions of his *salle d'armes*, it would seem that the Colonel's fascination with unusual and antiquated arms and armor continued until end of his days. In 1896, a reporter visiting his academy at the Schiller Building, in Chicago, observed:

The walls are covered from floor to ceiling with trophies of war in many countries. There are armor and weapons brought to Central and South America by the followers of Cortez, lances that have been bathed in blood in South American revolutions, priceless old Toledo blades, daggers, Cuban machetes, quaint old guns and pistols, and similar arms of the latest pattern, swords from every country where such weapons are made, fencing foils and masks, and military accoutrements.[81]

Perhaps Monstery truly was, as his biographer wondered, "born a few hundred years too late, a genuine son of chivalry stepped down into the middle of the nineteenth century."[82]

A Professor of Sparring

Although he was principally known as a fencing master, Monstery offered additional instruction in unarmed self-defense—advertised as "sparring" or "boxing," but which also involved grappling, as well as how to defend against kicking, butting, and other natural weapons. In a printed circular advertising his "School at Arms," Monstery noted,

> The pupils of Col. Monstery obtain a superior degree of proficiency, and his course in boxing is the most complete extant, and includes all the tactics that are necessary in the art. He has long made the offensive part his special study, so that the pupil will not injure his hands, instead of his opponent, should he engage in an encounter with boxing gloves off, in his own defense.[83]

Monstery's fencing events often included contests and demonstrations of boxing, *savate*, and various styles of British wrestling.[84] He was also known to arrange bare-knuckle fights at his school during after hours, helping combatants settle their disputes in the old-fashioned manner.[85] Luminaries of the boxing and wrestling world, such as Mike Donovan, William Miller, André Christol, and William Muldoon (the trainer of John L. Sullivan), are recorded as having visited Monstery's school.[86]

One day, around 1888 or 1889, a young amateur—a Chicago draftsman named Frank—entered Monstery's academy at the old Athenaeum, and engaged for a course of twelve boxing lessons. Frank, who had been the target of bullying and intimidation in his workplace, had "boxed some." Still, he admitted, he had not "much science." Frank told the Colonel that he "wanted to learn how to hit hard and stop body-blows," explaining that he could already protect his head. Monstery first tried to convince Frank to learn to fence with "the foils"—which were, he declared, more properly suited

Monstery teaching self-defense.

to gentlemen. Frank explained, "I'm not involved with gentlemen. I've got a battle on hand with a pretty tough bunch. I want some rough training." Monstery agreed, and handed Frank the gloves. The draftsman recounted,

I put them on and put up my guard. "No," [Monstery] said, "college boy! This way," and he put one hand down, the other out in front like a feeler and provocative. "Now, look out." He struck at me a number of times to see where I was. "Not so bad. Now, I'm going to hit you," he said. "Go ahead." He did, and the jolt jarred me to the heels. I thought if it was that easy to reach me I was far from [being ready] . . . Took the bout for an hour.

After two weeks of training under Monstery, Frank felt he could defend himself fairly well, and arranged for an impromptu boxing match with his bullying colleagues—in which he soundly defeated two of them back to back. Frank would later be required to defend himself against additional assaults, and describes using strikes, head-locks, and improvised weapons to emerge from these scrapes—all techniques that Monstery was known to have taught. Although Frank Lloyd Wright would never achieve fame as a pugilist, he would go on to become a highly successful architect.[87]

TRAINING FOR DUELS

While Monstery's training was intended to promote physical and mental discipline, help his students excel in contests of skill, and prepare them for street defense, it also occasionally served another serious purpose—preparation for the duel.[88] Although, during the late nineteenth century, dueling was no longer encouraged or con-doned by American society at large, duels still occurred, being fought primarily by members of the American fencing subculture and Euro-pean immigrants. Every once in a while, Monstery would receive a request for training from a person embroiled in an "affair of honor." One such episode was recounted in detail in the pages of the *Colum-bus Journal*:

[Monstery] was sitting in his office in New York one gloomy eve-ning in 1871, when there was a nervous knock on the door. "Come in," cried he, and on the invitation there entered a young man, who proved on inquiry to be one Col. Canzi, a soldier of the days of

Garibaldi, who immediately began to unfold the tale of his plight. He was under contract, it seemed, to fight at dawn with Gen. Fardella, also a tried and courageous veteran. The weapons to be used were sabers, and Canzi knew about as much of handling a saber as he did of cooking a Welsh rarebit. He needed sleep badly, and two hours was all he had in which to learn enough to save his life.

Those blessed two hours the colonel employed in teaching him two vicious cuts, either one of which, if well delivered, was calculated to cut off his adversary in his prime. He was told to bide his time, wear the general out by defensive tactics, and then send his cut home at the proper moment. Canzi departed full of hope, and followed out his orders to the letter. After twenty minutes of hard fighting, during which he successfully repelled Fardella's attacks, he delivered one of his two cuts with such conscientious effect that the general's sword arm was slit clear from elbow to wrist, completely disabling him.[89]

The fee that Monstery charged for preparing Canzi for this combat was both generous and shrewd. When the Italian asked him his price, Monstery replied:

> If you are wounded, nothing. If you win the duel, pay me according to what you think your life is worth.[90]

Unfortunately, there seems to be no record of exactly what amount Canzi decided upon.

Monstery was regarded as an authority on dueling not only by would-be duelists, but also by members of the press. In 1888, after French Prime Minister Charles Floquet defeated General Boulanger with a sword-thrust to the neck in a widely publicized duel, a journalist approached the Colonel to obtain his thoughts. Monstery's response gives further insight into his views on the mind-set and technique of dueling:

Gen. Boulanger... from what I learn by the papers, brought about his defeat by his lack of coolness and consequent fury of attack. He rushed blindly on his foe, losing all sight of prudence and skill in the desire to inflict injury. For an expert swordsman to overcome such an attack is an easy matter. He has only to wait coolly for his antagonist to leave an opening and then sail in... Between you and me, I think Boulanger was in great luck. A man who employs the tactics he did in the presence of a skillful swordsman will be killed in nine cases out of ten.[91]

Oftentimes, Monstery would refuse to train would-be duelists, especially if he believed that malice was a motivating factor between the parties involved. In fact, the Colonel would only grant these requests after receiving a promise that the knowledge "should not be used to kill the adversary." He explained,

I keep my secrets for the use of the weak against the strong, not to enable men to injure each other.[92]

This view not only sums up Monstery's attitude toward dueling, but pervades his whole martial philosophy as expressed throughout the years.

Attitudes Toward Health and Physical Education

Monstery was also notable as a fencing master in that he was highly cognizant of the mind-body connection, a concept which he often emphasized in his interviews and writings. Monstery believed that the consistent practice of fencing over one's lifetime had a profoundly positive effect on one's health—preventing disease, lengthening life, and promoting strength and vitality. One of his mottos was, "He who lives by the sword lives long."[93] In 1878, an athlete suffering from chronic weakness and fatigue wrote to Monstery seeking advice. He had tried numerous medicines as well as physical exercises such as gymnastics in an attempt to alleviate his condition, but to no avail. In his response to the sufferer, Monstery advocated a complete change of lifestyle with "continual activity of mind and body," explaining:

> Medicine, and the so-called "training down" [weight reduction], are the two deadly foes to the human system. You have, thereby, for years directed the nourishment you have received to the external man, at the expense of the inner or vital portion. In your case, medicine will only injure. Nature, alone, will restore you.[94]

Monstery believed that certain activities tended to impart longevity toward the practitioner, the chief among these being boxing, riding, swimming, and calisthenics. Above all these he placed the art of fencing, elucidating:

> It seems to have a strange influence on the body, improving the quality of the muscles and nerves . . . I have found such extraordinary power developed by fencing in bodies not by any means muscular, the muscles not feeling very hard to the touch, that I cannot help attributing the strength to something apart from muscle, and residing in the will force of the nerves and brain.[95]

In a booklet advertising his "School at Arms," Monstery further noted that fencing

> creates a glow, and it infuses in pupils a vital energy, which enables them to perform the mind's labor with ease and without exhausting the body. It rejuvenates the body and electrifies the mind. To either youth or middle age, or even old age, it imparts a vitality that no other course will attain.[96]

Toward the end of his life, Monstery's enduring strength and vigor, reported by many observers, became a testament to this philosophy. It should be noted that the Colonel's theory is supported by numerous anecdotes in the annals of fencing history, which tell of masters who continued to fence with amazing skill up until the last week of their lives, sometimes to an extraordinary age.[97] The treatise of Cesar Enrichetti, for instance, tells of an Italian master named Bartolomeo Bertolini, who gave a fencing exhibition in Milan at age 100 which "astonished all who witnessed such agility united with such age," and who lived to the advanced age of 105.[98] While Monstery did not live nearly so long, the following incident in his life, which occurred in 1892, illustrates his unusual powers for a man of sixty-eight years. While walking down a Chicago street corner, he was ambushed and assaulted by two thugs, who had evidently set their sights on Monstery's pocket watch. After receiving a punch to his side, the Colonel recovered from the shock of the initial attack and began to defend himself:

> His first blow laid out one of his assailants and reduced the contest to a man-for-man struggle. When it was over the Colonel's hands were covered with the other fellow's blood, and he was uninjured, save for a scratch on the side of his face, where one of the thugs had pulled out a portion of his mustache.[99]

This apparent strength and vitality would continue for about a decade. Monstery's life came to an end just a few months prior to his seventy-seventh birthday—not a remarkable lifespan by modern standards, but significantly higher than the average life expectancy of his generation.[100] Only a month before his death, a reporter noted that Monstery did "not look a day over fifty and is still wonderfully athletic and with the exception of slightly failing eyesight is just about as good a swordsman as he ever was."[101]

MONSTERY'S TREATISE

Although Colonel Monstery is no longer with us, his martial wisdom survives in an obscure, forgotten treatise entitled *Physical Education for Gentlemen*, published in serial form in *The Spirit of the Times*, a New York–based magazine that catered to the tastes of upper-class sportsmen. In October of 1877, the *Spirit* announced that

> Among special [upcoming] features will be a series of articles, entitled *Physical Education for Gentlemen*, from the pen of one whose reputation as a master of all arms is worldwide. Principally noted as a swordsman, Col. Thomas H. Monstery has distinguished himself in the various countries of Europe, where assaults-at-arms are still practiced, as one of the best fencers of modern times . . . Col. Monstery is an enthusiast in his chosen profession, and has carried the science of physical education to a perfection such as few men, living or dead, have attained.
>
> The series will begin with a general treatise on physical education, followed by full lessons on boxing, foil-fencing, broadsword or stick, knife play, and The Art of Swimming . . . This sounds incredible, but facts support the claim, and we congratulate the readers of *The Spirit* on the treat in store for them.[102]

This description of the treatise's contents would not prove very accurate; Monstery never included a section on foil fencing, although his opening chapter did discuss fencing in a general context. Nor would there appear the promised chapter on knife fighting. In its place, however, Monstery included something perhaps even more special and historically significant: a section on the quarterstaff.

Monstery's treatise is highly unique for several reasons. First, it is one of only a few nineteenth-century treatises that presents a system of boxing intended purely for self-defense—not for use in the ring.

Originally, in previous centuries, boxing had developed as a bare-knuckle martial art intended both for self-defense and the settling of disputes.[103] By the late nineteenth century, however, the focus and objective of boxing had largely shifted to winning at gloved competition—even though its techniques were still often taught under the pretext of "self-defense."[104] As one author of the period explained, modern boxing had become

the mere shadow and semblance of what it was formerly. Fifty years ago sparring with the gloves was regarded chiefly as a means to an end. The teacher of it instructed his pupil, not with a view of enabling him to use the glove prettily, but how to use his fist with most effect. The critic looking on at an encounter in Bendigo's rooms estimated the value of each blow, not at all by the effect it had when delivered with the gloved fist, but by the effect it would have produced if the glove had not been there. Sparring was then the mere science underlying the more practical art of pugilism. It has now usurped both titles, and is considered more often as the end than as the means. Now and then, it is true, we find a man going to learn boxing because he thinks "it may be useful to him in a street row"; but the far greater part of those who now take lessons do so purely with the desire of excelling in competitions with the gloves. Half the men who win the most honours and prizes in these competitions have never struck a blow with the bare fist since they were at school, and are little likely to do so till the day of their death.[105]

Monstery, however, unambiguously states in chapter nine of his treatise,

I am not writing for or teaching prize-fighters. I am teaching gentlemen how to defend themselves if assaulted by ruffians, and how to take useful exercise with their friends with gloves on.

Because his system was ultimately intended for self-defense without gloves, Monstery advocates a guard position somewhat different than those found in other treatises of the period, with a raised right hand and a lowered, more withdrawn left hand, as well as a lightly placed left foot that "can be drawn back in case of a kick made at it":

Monstery's boxing system is also notable in that it is partly based on fencing theory. The Colonel discussed this at length in an interview given nearly ten years after the publication of his treatise, in which he states:

Success all lies in knowing how to hit—to establish a line of power from the shoulder to the knuckles of the second, third and forefingers. The principle is the same in fencing. Let me take a foil and deliver a thrust glancing downward and the point will only scratch you, whereas if I deliver a thrust with the "line of power" behind it,

Monstery's guard (1878). *Richard Kyle Fox's guard (1889).*

the bones and muscles all backing each other with cumulative force, the foil would go right through you.

I discovered the scientific blow that Sullivan uses—his "knock-out" blow. It remained for a man thoroughly acquainted with the art of fencing to discover this blow, which is produced exactly like a thrust in *tierce*, see? A blow so dealt by a powerful man will stun an ox, and a scientific lightweight or gentleman amateur can by means of it hold his own against any slugger in the ring who is unfamiliar with the principle. A man who is an accomplished fencer is invariably a good boxer; not because sword practice develops a quick eye and general activity, but because his cuts and thrusts when used with the fist as the weapon are the most powerful and effective blows that can be used on an opponent.[106]

In addition to the chapters on striking, Monstery includes sections on grappling, headlocks, trips, back-falls, and the use of "natural weapons" such as the head and feet. He offers detailed, practical advice on how to deal with "malicious boxers," and for handling oneself in street encounters. He also discusses how to defend against other fighting styles of the era, such as French *savate*, British "purring" (shin-kicking), Welsh jump-kicking, Danish head-fighting, African American head-butting, and rough-and-tumble fighting—a particularly brutal American style which involved grappling, kicking, biting, scratching, and eye-gouging.[107] To this author's knowledge, Monstery's treatise is the only piece of extant literature that discusses in detail how to defend against these last five fighting styles.

After covering unarmed self-defense, Monstery's treatise proceeds to the cane, which he describes as one of the best and most practical weapons for street self-defense, effective against sticks, knives, sword-canes, and even guns.

The final section of Monstery's treatise deals with the quarter-staff. Monstery begins by discussing the *Alpenstock*, or Germanic-Danish version of the staff, which was still practiced as a living tradition during his own time, being taught to the peasant militias of Denmark and Northern Germany "for use in case of riot against mobs." Although Monstery was trained to use the weapon while enrolled at the Royal Military Institute at Copenhagen, he refers to the system presented in his text as "the modern staff-exercise," described as "a little different" than the old British style. Whether the system he presents is a version of the Germanic-Danish tradition, or is something else that other fencing masters were teaching during the era, is difficult to say. If we are to take the word of the *Spirit*'s editors, then the former would seem to be the case, as they prefaced Monstery's chapter with the announcement that he would give "instruction in the use of the *Alpenstock* as a weapon this week." Whatever the case, it is one of only a handful of quarterstaff treatises still in existence, and the only one published in America prior to the twentieth century.[108]

While the editors of *The Spirit of the Times* predicted that Monstery's articles would become "the standard work" on the subject, his treatise was, for reasons unknown, never published in book form.[109] For a time, the *Spirit* offered pamphlets on request containing Monstery's chapters on boxing and swimming, but none on fencing with the cane or quarterstaff. Since then, his treatise has spent the last 130 years buried in oblivion, during which time Monstery's fame and prowess as a martial artist has been all but forgotten.

With the present publication, it is hoped that the Colonel's insight, wisdom, and techniques may now finally reach a larger audience, as he no doubt originally intended.

Endnotes

1 *New York Sun*, Feb. 6, 1881, 6.

2 *Chicago Daily Tribune*, July 27, 1892, 2.

3 Baptism record, Copenhagen, Denmark, 1824–1826. It is worth noting that numerous contemporary sources erroneously state that Monstery was born in Baltimore, Maryland—an error that may have originated with, or at least seems to have been encouraged by, Monstery himself.

4 H. S. Canfield, "Monstery: Soldier of Fortune," *Everybody's Magazine* 7, no. 4 (Oct. 1902): 330.

5 Vivat Victorius Fridericus Franciscus Nachetgall (1777–1847), Director of the Royal Military Institute at Copenhagen, widely regarded as the founder of physical education in Denmark.

6 *Utica Saturday Globe*, Aug. 10, 1895.

7 The Comte de Montrichard and M. Beurnier, two French émigrés in exile, instructed Ling in Copenhagen according to R. Schenström, *Gymnastique médicale suédoise: Traitement des maladies chroniques, Méthode Ling* (Paris: 26, Avenue Friedland, 18[?]). Ling studied under these two masters between 1799 and 1804; eventually Montrichard "gave him a paper which certified to his great skill with the foil and his ability to give instruction in the art." George Wells Fitz, *American Physical Education Review* 9 (Boston: American Physical Education Association, 1904): 228–229. As to the identity of the first-mentioned master, by process of elimination he is almost certainly the same Louis-Henry-François-Gabriel-Ferdinand, Comte de Montrichard, mentioned in the *Etat Présent de la Noblese Française*. A member of the *Ancien Régime*, and a former "Gentleman of the King's House," he was admitted to the knighthood of St. George in 1781, and served as an officer of the La Sarre regiment of infantry; later he was promoted to captain of the Royal Dragoons, Marshal-General-master of the camps and armies of the King, attached to the staff of the army, captain in the constitutional mounted guard of King Louis XVI in 1791. Died in Paris, 1830. Baron Henry de Woelmont, *Notices généalogiques: Quatrième série* (Paris: 1928), 572.

8 N. Strömborg, *Gymnastiklära: efter P.H. Ling och G. Branting. Första häftet, Fäktlära* (Stockholm: F. E. Östlund, 1857); and Gustaf Nyblæus, *Fäktlära* (Stockholm: P. A. Norstedt & Soner, 1876), 8–208.

9 Canfield, "Monstery: Soldier of Fortune," 330.

10 Capt. Frederick Whittaker, *The Sword Prince: The Romantic Life of Col. Monstery, American Champion-at-Arms* (New York: M. J. Ivers & Co., 1884), 6.

11 John J. Flinn, ed., *The Handbook of Chicago Biography* (Chicago: The Standard Guide Company, 1893), 260.

12 Whittaker, *The Sword Prince*.

13 *New York Sun*, Apr. 9, 1899, 6.

14 Ibid.

15 Whittaker, *The Sword Prince*, 25.

16 *New York Sun*, Apr. 9, 1899, 6.

17 *St. Paul Daily Globe*, May 27, 1888, 12.

18 Whittaker, *The Sword Prince*, 21.

19 Canfield, "Monstery: Soldier of Fortune," 335.

20 In fencing terminology, a time-thrust.

21 *St. Paul Daily Globe*, May 27, 1888.

22 Whittaker, *The Sword Prince*, 7.

23 *Chicago Daily Tribune*, July 27, 1892, 2.

24 Whittaker, *The Sword Prince*, 27.

25 Whittaker, *The Sword Prince*, 30.

26 Whittaker, *The Sword Prince*, 29. Of the fatal duel in Mexico, Monstery merely recounted: "May 23, 1868, I was forced into a duel which caused me to kill my opponent, and I had to retire precipitately." *Utica Saturday Globe*, Aug. 10, 1895.

27 Whittaker, *The Sword Prince*, 30.

28 Whittaker, *The Sword Prince*, 16–18.

29 According to various newspapers and city directories, Monstery arrived in New York City in 1870, and began teaching at Arbor Hall, 50 West Houston Street. In 1871 he opened a school at 26 West Fourth Street;

then moved it to 55 Bleecker Street, and again to 18 Clinton Place, where he remained until 1874. He then moved his academy to 619 Sixth Avenue, where he taught fencing, boxing, and ran a shooting gallery. In 1879, he was also teaching "Physical Culture" at the Hellenic Institute at 1481 Broadway. In 1880–81 he was listed at 811 Sixth Avenue. By 1884 he had moved his school to Chicago, where he remained until his death. See Albert Johannsen, *The House of Beadle and Adams and its Dime and Nickel Novels, Vol. 2* (Norman: University of Oklahoma Press, 1962), 202. *New York Clipper*, Sep. 24, 1870. *New York Herald*, Sep. 17, 1871. *New York Tribune*, Mar. 13, 1879, 6. In 1868, during a sojourn abroad, Monstery also opened an "Academia de Esgrima" in Mexico City, where he offered lessons in the "Florete, Espada, Sable de Infanteria, Sable de Caballeria, Esgrima de Bayoneta, Juego de Puñal, y Box." *El Monitor Republicano*, Feb. 15, 1868.

30 *Chicago Daily Tribune*, Nov. 10, 1893, 5. Monstery also presided over such contests as a judge, always attempting to ensure that the sword was treated as a serious weapon. In an 1893 contest, it was noted that "To an outsider it looked very much as if every time one man would hit the other, the struck one would cross-counter in a splendid style, returning the blow with interest. This, however, was decided by those who were up in the sport to be against the tenets of swordsmanship. 'For,' argued Colonel Monstery, 'If the weapons were sharp the first blow struck would cut off the head of him who received it, and how could a man with his head cut off return a stroke?'" *Daily Inter Ocean*, Nov. 3, 1893.

31 *New York Sun*, Jan. 6, 1880.

32 *New York Herald*, Mar. 7, 1876.

33 "Col. Monstery's Right to the Championship," *Turf, Field, and Farm*, Mar. 31, 1876. "The Arms Tournament," *Turf, Field, and Farm*, Apr. 14, 1876. *Army and Navy Journal*, Apr. 15, 1876.

34 *New York Times*, Apr. 11, 1876, and *Army and Navy Journal*, Apr. 15, 1876.

35 *New York Times*, Jan. 5, 1880.

36 Francis Wilson, *Recollections of a Player* (New York: De Vinne Press, 1897), 26.

37 *Daily Inter Ocean*, Feb. 25, 1891.

38 *Spirit of the Times*, Jan. 12, 1878.

39 *Daily Inter Ocean*, Feb. 25, 1891.

40 *Spirit of the Times*, Jan. 12, 1878.

41 *Daily Inter Ocean*, Feb. 25, 1891.

42 Francis Wilson, *Francis Wilson's Life of Himself* (Boston and New York: Houghton Mifflin Company, 1924), 46–47; Wilson, *Recollections of a Player*, 25.

43 Wilson, *Life of Himself*, 131.

44 *New York Sun*, Feb. 6, 1881, 6.

45 "By the Broadsword Route," *New York Times*, Apr. 29, 1906. Contrary to what the *New York Times* states, some sources declare that Hattan began training with Monstery at age twenty in Chicago (see, for instance, *Macon Telegraph*, May 27, 1906). However, given Hattan's year of birth (1859), whether she began at age eighteen or twenty, Monstery would still have been living and teaching in New York City.

46 "Sword's Queen," *Boston Daily Globe*, Sept. 29, 1892, 4; "Jaguarina Going Into Vaudeville," *Washington Post*, Feb. 21, 1897, 18; "The Ways of Jaguarina," *New York Times*, Apr. 11, 1897; "She Defeated 60 Men," *Boston Daily Globe*, May 31, 1897, 9; "By the Broadsword Route," *New York Times*, Apr. 29, 1906; "Chatting with the Porter in 'The Vanderbilt Cup,'" *New York Evening Telegram*, May 7, 1906.

47 "Jaguarine. A Quiet Little Chat with the Pretty 'Amazon,'" *Los Angeles Times*, July 13, 1887.

48 "She Defeated 60 Men," 9.

49 *Cleveland Plain Dealer*, Apr. 10, 1898.

50 *New York Sunday Telegraph*, Dec. 20, 1903.

51 *Cleveland Plain Dealer*, Apr. 10, 1898.

52 *Victoria Daily Colonist*, Mar. 11, 1893.

53 *Los Angeles Herald*, Nov. 28, 1890.

54 *Cleveland Plain Dealer*, Apr. 10, 1898.

55 *New York Sunday Telegraph*, Dec. 20, 1903.

56 A flurry of articles appearing in the United States during the late 1890s announced fencing as the new fashionable activity for women. See "Smart Set Fencing," *Boston Daily Globe*, May 31, 1896; "Fencing Now Society's Fad," *New York Times*, May 2, 1897; "Take Up the Foils, Madame," *New York Sun*, Jan. 18, 1903; "Fencing from the Standpoint of Physical Culture," *San Francisco Call*, July 18, 1909; "Most Skillful of Women Fencers to Meet," *New York Sun*, Mar. 17, 1912.

57 *New York Sun*, Feb. 6, 1881, 6.

58 "Maids of Muscle," *Weekly Inter Ocean*, Nov. 30, 1886, 5.

59 *Omaha World Herald*, Nov. 2, 1890, 6.

60 *New York Sunday Telegraph*, Apr. 15, 1900.

61 *Auburn Daily Bulletin*, Mar. 16, 1891.

62 *New York Sun*, Feb. 6, 1881, 6.

63 Ibid.

64 "Maids of Muscle," 5.

65 *New York Sun*, Feb. 6, 1881, 6.; *The Current* 7, no. 179 (May 21, 1887): 711; *Omaha Daily Bee*, Jan. 3, 1888, 5.; *Auburn Daily Bulletin*, Mar. 16, 1891.

66 *Western Medical Reporter*, June, 1881, 141.

67 *New York Sun*, Feb. 6, 1881, 6.

68 *Daily Inter Ocean*, Apr. 22, 1888.

69 "Foils in Feminine Hands," 1.; *Pittsburgh Press*, Apr. 26, 1888.

70 *Daily Alta California*, Apr. 7, 1861.

71 *Daily Alta California*, Nov. 28, 1863, 1.

72 *Daily Morning Call*, Aug. 4, 1864.

73 Monstery's three rapier contests were fought against Emile Verbouiviens, Regis Senac, and Captain De Turck. See *New York Times*, Mar. 10, 1876 and Apr. 11, 1876, and *New York Herald*, May 28, 1879. Although Monstery was challenged in print to a fourth contest with "the rapier, cut and thrust" by J. Rein [José Recio] Betancourt, it is unclear if this event ever materialized. See *New York Herald*, Mar. 16, 1880.

74 Several Italian fencing treatises of the nineteenth century attest to this. Blasco Florio (1844) describes the Italian sword (*spada*) as having "two cutting edges," two flat sides, and a sharp point. He also states that the blade used in Sicily is pyramidal-quadrangular, with fine cutting edges and a sharp point. The treatise of Alberto Marchionni (1847) contains an illustration of a fencer in the Neapolitan guard, holding a cup-hilt rapier with cross-bar, quillions, and knuckle-bow, and with his left hand poised in front of the chest to deviate the adversary's blade. Vittorio Lambertini (1870) describes the blade of the Italian sword as being quadrangular in form, "but there are some blades that are larger and flattened, narrowing proportionately to the point. These are used chiefly in duels, where both the point and cut are employed." See William H. Gaugler, *The History of Fencing* (Bangor: Laureate Press, 1998), 113–114, 116, 147, 170.

The corpus of evidence attesting to the survival of Spanish rapier fencing is so vast that it cannot be included here, and shall be covered in a future work. However, an 1897 article summarized the survival of the school as follows: "Up to the middle of the eighteenth century most of the great teachers of Europe outside of their own country were Italians. Now almost the only surviving schools of the old systems are the Neapolitan, Bolognese and at Madrid where is yet to be seen the dagger in the left hand as an aid and guard to the rapier in the right hand." See "Fencing as an Exercise," *Detroit Free Press*, Oct 17, 1897.

75 *Daily Inter Ocean*, Apr. 18, 1887; *Turf, Field, and Farm*, Mar. 24, 1876.

76 *Courrier des États-Unis*, Jan. 4, 1880, 2.

77 *New York Herald*, Mar. 16, 1880. Monstery would later accept this challenge, agreeing to "his choice of the rapier." *New York Herald*, Mar. 18, 1880. Although it is unclear if this event ever materialized, the two had contested six years before: "Col Monstery then introduced Gen. Betancourt, and in this assault an entirely distinct school was again fully illustrated. It was *L'Espada Espagnol*—no quarter, no rule, but do the best you can, and may the best man win. Gen Betancourt is a man of powerful

build, yet withal exceedingly rapid, and at all times showing the calmness and confidence acquired by long familiarity with the sword and danger." *Turf, Field, and Farm*, Jan. 16, 1874.

78 *New York Times*, Dec. 27, 1883. *New York Sun*, Apr. 6, 1884, 6.

79 *New York Times*, June 11, 1895.

80 The participants in this event were later identified as Captain Juillard and Léon Caton, both from the Cavalry School of Saumur, France; Prof. Louis Friedrich of the New York Turnverein, M.M. De Turck of Wood's Gymnasium, Prof. William Miller of Australia, Prof. James McGregor of London, Señor Martinez, Emile Verbouiviens, French Græco-Roman wrestler and pugilist André Christol ("the tiger of the Pyrenees"), Col. Monstery himself, and Monstery's son, Emilio. Dr. P. Allen also read a paper on "Physical Culture," and Monstery's wife, Carmen Xiques Monstery, performed on the piano. The event took place at the old Lyceum Theatre (formerly the Theatre Francais) at 107 Fourteenth Street. *New York Times*, Mar. 3, 1876. *Turf, Field, and Farm*, Mar. 3, 1876. *Courrier des États-Unis*, Mar. 8, 1876. *Daily Graphic*, Mar. 10, 1876. *New York Times*, Mar. 10, 1876. *Turf, Field, and Farm*, Mar. 17, 1876. *New York Herald*, Oct. 19, 1879.

81 *Chicago Daily Tribune*, Feb. 2, 1896, 38.

82 Whittaker, *The Sword Prince*, 31.

83 From a copy of a booklet entitled "Col. T. H. Monstery, School at Arms" in the possession of Monstery descendent Diane Hayes.

84 *Daily Alta California*, Nov. 28, 1863, 1; *New York Clipper*, June 20, 1874; *New York Herald*, Mar. 21, 1879. *Omaha World Herald*, Oct. 16, 1888

85 *Cleveland Leader*, Feb. 3, 1888.

86 *Courrier des États-Unis*, Mar. 8, 1876. *New York Clipper*, Mar. 3, 1877. *New York Times*, May 19, 1878. *Denver Post*, Apr. 15, 1913.

87 Frank Lloyd Wright, *Frank Lloyd Wright: An Autobiography* (New York: Duell, Sloan and Pearce, 1943), 98–100.

88 Monstery noted, "[fencing] familiarizes the mind with danger . . . and accustoms one to look with calmness on the dangers of life." *Daily Alta*

California, Apr. 7, 1861. Monstery also trained his "dear friend Aquillara and his son for a duel." *Daily Inter Ocean*, Oct. 11, 1895.

89 *Columbus Journal*, Aug. 29, 1888, 4. A detailed account of this duel, published in the *Cincinatti Daily Enquirer*, Sept. 5, 1871, confirms all the major details of Monstery's story, notes that the combat took place in Williamsburg, Brookyln, and vividly describes the duel's climax: "General Fardelli wielded his huge saber with great power but with little precision. His adversary was decidedly the cooler of the two, and it was not long before this fact began to tell . . . Both gentlemen strove to make home cuts and thrusts, but the guards were too well covered. But Fardelli was too violent. At last he made a desperate effort to cut Colonel Canzi's leg. He swung his saber with a peculiar flourish, and as he made a feint at Canzi's head in order to uncover the latter's leg guard, he unluckily left his own arm exposed . . . the saber took a quick sweep and went crashing through the General's arm. It cut clean from the shoulder to the wrist, and laid it open to the bone."

90 Whittaker, *The Sword Prince*, 29.

91 *Columbus Journal*, Aug. 29, 1888, 4.

92 Whittaker, *The Sword Prince*, 28–29.

93 Canfield, "Monstery: Soldier of Fortune," 329.

94 *Spirit of the Times*, Jan. 12, 1878.

95 See chapter 1 of this book.

96 From a copy of a booklet entitled "Col. T. H. Monstery, School at Arms" in the possession of Monstery descendent Diane Hayes.

97 For anecdotes of fencing masters' longevity, see "Extract of a Letter from Henry Angelo, Esq; of Bolton Row, May Fair. Dated London, October 19, 1806" in Sir John Sinclair, *The Code of Health and Longevity*, Vol. II (Edinburgh: Arch. Constable & Co., 1807), 162–64.

98 Gaugler, *History of Fencing*, 182, 460.

99 *Daily Inter Ocean*, Oct. 15, 1892.

100 Monstery was born in 1824. As of 1850, American males born in 1820 could expect to live to age sixty-four, while the average life expectancy

of those born in 1830 was sixty-one. Source: U.S. Dept. of Commerce, Bureau of the Census, *Historical Statistics of the United States*.

101 *Mexican Herald*, Dec. 20, 1900.

102 *Spirit of the Times*, Oct. 27, 1877, 346.

103 For example, see Thomas Fewtrell, *Boxing Reviewed; or, the Science of Manual Defence* (London: Scatcherd and Whitaker: 1790), 3–5, 40–41.

104 Contrast, for instance, Fewtrell with Richard Kyle Fox, *Boxing: With Hints on the Art of Attack and Defense and How to Train for the Prize Ring* (New York: Richard K. Fox, 1889). One boxing veteran of the period, William Madden, further explained: "You cannot compare the fighter of the past with those of today. Like several other things, yesterday is better than today. And the reason therefore is that the old timer hit straight punches. He could not swing as today, because he had nothing on his hands to save him. A straight puncher, therefore, is superior to any man who swings. Today glove-fighting is like sandbagging. You hit a man in the right place and he drops dizzy and unconscious . . . [in the past] it was the artist in those days that gave the straight punches, and it was the artist that won the fight." *Cleveland Plain Dealer*, Sept. 24, 1893.

105 *A New Book of Sports. Reprinted from the Saturday Review* (London: R. Bentley and Son, 1885), 126–135. This passage continues, "Accordingly, the spectators at an assault of arms, which is now the favourite occasion for a display of pugilistic science, no longer try to imagine what each blow would be like if the glove was off when it was delivered. They count the hits, not for what they represent, but for what they are; and thus often a loud-sounding slap with the half-open glove is applauded as a most telling stroke, while the neat 'upper cut,' which would tell ten times more heavily in a real battle, passes comparatively unnoticed and possibly unseen except by a few."

106 *Macon Telegraph*, Jan. 6, 1887. At least one firsthand account testifies to the efficacy of these strikes. When a young Frank Lloyd Wright—already a seasoned amateur boxer—began a series of sparring lessons under Monstery, he ended up on the receiving end of one of Monstery's

blows. Wright recounted, "the jolt jarred me to the heels." Wright, *An Autobiography*, 98–100.

107 For a brief overview of this fighting style as it was practiced in the American South, see Elliot Gorn, "Gouge and Bite, Pull Hair and Scratch," *The American Historical Review* 90 (Feb. to Dec. 1985): 18–43.

108 Although the Chicago-based instructor Giuseppe Riboni published a book in 1862 entitled "Broadsword and Quarter-staff," the staff weapon treated of is actually the Italian *bastone a dui mani*. See Giuseppe Riboni, *Broadsword and quarter-staff without a master: broadsword fencing and stick or quarter-staff play, after the latest European practice adopted in the military schools of France and Italy, and the United States* (Chicago: E. B. Myers: 1862).

109 Approximately nine months after his treatise appeared in the *Spirit*, a reader named "J. M." wrote the magazine asking if Monstery had published a work on fencing or boxing. An editor responded: "Col. Monstery has not published a book on either of these subjects, but has written articles on boxing for *The Spirit of the Times*, copies of which we can furnish you for $1.35." *Spirit of the Times*, Dec. 28, 1878, 548. See also Col. Thomas H. Monstery, *New Manual of the Art of Swimming, as Taught by the Monstery Method* (New York: The Spirit of the Times, 1878).

A NOTE TO THE READER

Monstery's treatise originally appeared as a series of articles covering a variety of self-defense methods, as well as the art of swimming. Since the present version includes only Monstery's combative material (having eliminated the section on swimming), and considering the fact that Monstery was such a strong advocate for the martial instruction of women (and, notably, includes some brief instruction specific to ladies in chapter 11), the title has been amended to *Self-Defense for Gentlemen and Ladies.*

The original version of Monstery's treatise included illustrations in the sections on boxing, fencing with the cane, and the quarterstaff. For the present version, some of the other chapters have been supplemented with period photographs, line drawings, and engravings. Chapter endnotes and a glossary of technical terms have also been added.

In preparing the present edition, the editor has attempted to be as faithful as possible to Monstery's original text. Typographical errors have been corrected, and antiquated spelling and punctuation have been updated where it was judged to be otherwise distracting to the reader. Where it was not deemed distracting, antiquated spelling and punctuation have been left intact.

Finally, it should be noted that in perusing Monstery's text, the modern reader may encounter comments that he or she may interpret as exhibiting a certain class or race prejudice. However, it is important to understand these passages within their socio-cultural and historical context.

First, Monstery was writing for a journal that specifically catered to the tastes of upper-class sportsmen, and some of his comments clearly address that audience:

> A gentleman ought to be superior to a laborer physically as well as mentally, and especially he be at all times superior to a rowdy. (Chapter 2)

Although this passage might seem to demonstrate class elitism, it is important to note that prior to the twentieth century, it was believed by much of American and European society that "culture makes the individual," and Monstery, born into an aristocratic lineage, would have been no different. Centuries before, Baltasar Gracián had written that

> Every human being is born a barbarian, and only culture redeems them from the bestial. Culture makes the person, the more the better... Ignorance is rough, and nothing refines more than learning. But even this learning remains a crude affair if sloven. Not only does our understanding require polish, but our desires as well, and especially our conduct.[1]

Similar sentiments endured well into Monstery's era, but by that time, in the minds of many, the word "gentleman"—formerly implying a lofty social status—had become associated with the high standard of behavior expected from members of that class.[2]

Second, Monstery's blunt comments that there was "no science" in the technique of African American head-butters, that they "do not fight; they merely butt heads to try which is hardest," and that they were physically more resilient than other fighters, may, at first glance, strike the modern reader as racist. These statements are better understood, however, when read with the knowledge that African American head-butting contests were typically decided not by science or skill, but by physical endurance and the ability to withstand pain, as can be observed in the vast majority of historical accounts.[3] Regardless of how one interprets these comments, a thorough examination of Monstery's life and writings is simply not consistent with a charge of racism. In 1889, writing from Paris, Monstery enthusiastically described the city's multiculturalism, noting that,

> At last I am in the world's capital, a world in itself, in fact, for we can see in it representatives of all quarters of the globe. I sat at a café table with a Turk, rode on an omnibus top with a Hindoo, borrowed a cigar light from an Arab, accidentally poked a Japanese count with my walking-stick, and am already on speaking terms with several Italians, Spaniards, Irishmen, Australians, Johnny Bulls, Zulus, Chileans, Mexicans, Danes, etc . . . Met several old friends, and a renewal of their acquaintance under such pleasant auspices served to add much to the enjoyment of my sojourn here.[4]

It is also worth mentioning that throughout his treatise, Monstery habitually derides those fighting styles (and fighters) that, in his estimation, lack "science" and humanity. In this, he reserves his harshest judgment for combatants belonging to his own race, Danes and Norwegians ("the last are as bad as the first," Monstery writes), as well as rough-and-tumble fighters—who consisted almost exclusively of white males.

Endnotes

1 Baltasar Gracián, *The Art of Worldly Wisdom* (New York: Barnes & Noble, 2008), 41–2.

2 *Encyclopædia Brittanica: A Dictionary of Arts, Sciences, Literature and General Information, Vol. XI* (Cambridge: University Press, 1910), 605.

3 See, for instance, Henry Bibb, *Narrative of the Life and Adventures of Henry Bibb, an American Slave* (New York: printed by author, 1850); *Memphis Daily Avalanche*, Feb. 10, 1867; *San Francisco Bulletin*, Oct. 23, 1874; *National Police Gazette*, Aug. 9, 1879; *St. Paul Daily Globe*, May 14, 1885; *Critic-Record*, April 25, 1889; *Sacramento Daily Union*, Nov. 23, 1890; *National Police Gazette*, Feb. 4, 1893; and *San Francisco Chronicle*, Oct. 16, 1894.

4 *Daily Inter Ocean*, Sept. 9, 1889.

— PART TWO —

Self-Defense *for* Gentlemen *and* Ladies

by Col. Thomas H. Monstery,

*Graduate of the Royal Military Institute of Gymnastics and Arms
in Denmark, and Professor Ling's Central Gymnastic Institute of
Stockholm; Professor of Arms in Sweden, Denmark, Germany, Russia;
in the Service of Spain, Central and South America, and the Mexican
Republic; formerly of Baltimore, and late Eight Years Instructor
in the San Francisco Olympic Club.*

In this number appears the first of an important and valuable series of articles, entitled *Physical Education for Gentlemen*, prepared by the celebrated master-at-arms, Col. Thomas H. Monstery. This gentleman, both as practitioner and theorist, stands quite at the head of his profession in this city. As a swordsman his reputation is unrivalled, and extends to Europe, in all of which countries he has distinguished himself. He is proficient not only with the foils, but with the broadsword, the rapier, the bayonet, and the knife, is also a master of fence. He has also made other styles of exercise, such as boxing and swimming, a study, and has regarded them with a view to their hygienic advantages, as a remedial agent for diseases brought on by brain work and sedentary occupation. In fact, on all matters of physical education, outside of gymnastics and rowing, he is a high authority, and his present series of articles will constitute a standard work upon the subject.

—*The Spirit of the Times*, December 22, 1877

I.

INTRODUCTION.

In the earliest times known in history, the object of athletic exercise was the destruction of life. The hunter and the warrior were the ideal athletes of those days. But it so happened that these men, in pursuing their hardy, outdoor life, now in vigorous exercise, anon in lazy repose, found themselves enjoying the same splendid health of body and activity that belongs to the wild animal. They thought no more of it than do the lion and the eagle, types of vigor and power. As time went on, and civilization increased, men who abandoned the life of the hunter and warrior for that of the plodding plowman, the toiling artisan, the sedentary scholar and merchant, found that, with a different mode of life, they lost their health and became heirs to disease. Some of these diseases were the fruit of overwork, others of sedentary habits. The result was the same in both cases—disease.

Then came the old Greeks, the first people in the world who cultivated athletics for the sake of health and bodily vigor, and they found their reward in a beauty of body that has never since been excelled, perpetuated, as it is, in eternal marble and bronze.

After the fall of the Greek Republics, athletics fell into their old state, being applied by all nations to the same purpose—the destruction of life. The Romans had no public games and gymnasia; they had nothing but gladiators and soldiers, while the mass of the people displayed all the vices and diseases incident to civilization.

After the fall of the Roman Empire the systems of barbarous times prevailed once more, with the additions forced by the feudal system. The free and noble were hunters and warriors all their lives, while the plodding work of the agriculturist and artisan was done by the serfs and "villains," who were slaves attached to the soil.

The Scandinavian nations were especially conspicuous for this mode of life, and as they quickly overran all Europe, forcing the earlier German and Celtic tribes into subjection, their institutions survived the longest of any. These magnificent old Norsemen were all hunters and warriors, overflowing with health, strength, and courage, grand men to look on, brave and hardy, long-lived and sagacious; models of what men should be physically. Their fault was their pitiless ferocity, and the wrong ends to which they devoted all their health and strength, till the institution of chivalry.

Chivalry was the brightest light of the Middle Ages, softening its rough manners, dedicating strength and valor to the service of justice and truth, and can never be sufficiently praised. It has been the fashion in later times to deride chivalry, and to insist that the chevaliers of the middle ages were brutal and ignorant, but the men who express such opinions are very wide of the facts. The manners of the middle ages were rough and brutal, but not those of chivalry. Without chivalry, the Norsemen and Franks would have remained as they began, savages and barbarians. Chivalry slowly molded them into "gentlemen," as we now call them, and only gave way at last to civilization.

While they lasted, the exercises of chivalry produced two effects, physical and mental. Physically, they produced graceful and vigorous bodies: mentally, they tended to courage, generosity, and truth. When chivalry fell into disuse, before civilization and gunpowder, its exercises survived for many years, with the same beneficent effects, softening the face of warfare to humanity, and hardening the frames of those strong and active gentlemen of Europe who lived in the ages of Shakespeare and Milton. At the close of the seventeenth century they fell into further disuse, the only surviving trace being the practice of fencing with the small sword; and at the close of the eighteenth and the commencement of the present century, even that faded away into oblivion more and more under the influence of the increasing power of firearms.

But as everything in nature has its compensations, so in the affairs of nations. The chivalrous exercises, no longer necessary as a preparation for hand-to-hand fighting, have been resumed in modern times for the sake of their undoubted influence on health and longevity, and the Scandinavian races that peopled England and America have resumed the practice of athletics as ardently as the ancient Greeks, and for the same purpose. The whole of my life, owing to circumstances and a natural love for physical exercise, has been devoted to the cultivation of athletics, and I desire to give the American people, among whom that life has been spent, the benefit of all the experience that I have acquired on the subject.

First, I must remark that there are good systems of athletics that tend to health and long life, and bad ones, which tend to shorten life. The bad systems are those which overtask the strength by severe strains, requiring long "training," so called, to produce an artificial state of the system, fitted to endure the strain for a time. These systems are those which produce large muscles at the expense of vitality. Such are lifting heavy weights and dumb-bells, swinging heavy Indian clubs; exercising on the horizontal and parallel bars, where the body is supported by the arms, not the legs; rowing and running long races; walking against time, and every other exercise where the system is taxed to the utmost. Such exercises produce large muscles—too large for the heart and lungs behind them, too large for the vital force that moves them. They all tend to shorten the life.

The good systems are those which exercise the whole body simultaneously, rapidly, and for a short time tending to harden rather than enlarge the muscles, to make the tendons elastic, to increase the size of the thorax and lungs, quicken the circulation of the blood to a moderate extent, exercise the mind in conjunction with the body, and increase the flexibility of trunk and limbs. Such exercises tend to longevity and health. They are fencing, boxing, riding, swimming, and calisthenics. At the head of all I place fencing.

My reasons for placing fencing first are of two kinds, theoretical and practical. First, I hold that no exercise is good for the body, and likely to be pursued, if it does not influence and interest the mind. A "constitutional" walk along a road, a turn with the dumb-bells or clubs, tire the muscles, but do not exhilarate the mind, while a ramble across a beautiful country, a day's shooting or fishing, leave a pleasant impression on the mind, and make one forget fatigue. Hunters, and soldiers in campaign, with their minds on their work, are enthusiastic and healthy, and become more infatuated daily with their sport, whereas very few men can pursue heavy gymnastics for long without tiring of them, unless spurred by the emulation of a contest.

Fencing is one of those exercises that employs the mind as well as the body, and, in fact, employs it more than the body, the further a man advances in proficiency. From the first it supplies the excitement of contest, and depends so much on art and address that the man of superior mind always makes the best fencer in the end.

Physically, it employs every muscle of the body, as God meant they should be used, the man standing upright on his legs, not hanging by his arms, which were never meant to support his weight, or they would have been made as strong as the legs, like the arms of an ape or gorilla. I have tried, without success, to teach a monkey to fence, but no acrobat can climb like a monkey. These are the theoretical reasons that induce me to place fencing at the head of modern physical culture, as a means of preserving health. Particularly, I notice that the attitudes of modern fencing, on the system of which I shall hereafter speak, tend to arch the front of the chest, hollow the back, and enlarge the thorax, so as to encourage the lungs to expand.

My practical reasons are the result of my experience. I notice that men who practice heavy gymnastics young, who train for excessive races or prize fights, who lift weights or their own bodies as a constant thing, die young. Acrobats never live to an old age, unless they drop their profession.

Fencers, on the other hand, almost always live to a good old age. The great Swedish fencing-master, Ling[1], who introduced the modern style of fencing, first took to that exercise to save himself from consumption, being a slender, delicate man. He not only recovered his health, but became the first fencer in Europe, and gave an assault in public when he was past sixty years of age.[2] It is but seldom that a fencer dies of disease, whereas very few athletes die otherwise, in consequence of strains to the system or from heart disease.

Go to the dressing-room of any circus, and you will find the acrobats all pale and weary-looking men. Strip them, and their muscles will excite your admiration, but for my part I always pity the man that I see with exaggerated limbs, for I know that he gains his muscle at the expense of something else—his life—through the nerve system.

I find in my experience that fencing does not enlarge the muscles, but it makes what you have firm and elastic, and it strengthens

Ling

1776–1839

Dr. Pehr Henrik Ling.

the nerve system. It seems to have a strange influence on the body, improving the quality of the muscles and nerves. I even think that it may have some effect on the marrow of the bones, though, of course, on this point it is impossible to decide in the absence of experiment. Still, I have found such extraordinary power developed by fencing in bodies not by any means muscular, the muscles not feeling very hard to the touch, that I cannot help attributing the strength to something apart from muscle, and residing in the will force of the nerves and brain. No physician has yet offered any satisfactory explanation of the function of the marrow in the bones, and I cannot help a suspicion that my theory may be near the truth, though I do not offer it as anything more than a theory.

Besides this, from the constant stretching of the tendons, they become so elastic as to lessen the danger of ruptures and strains to a great degree. A man who fences constantly is not nearly so liable to sprain his wrist or ankle by sudden and violent exertion as one whose tendons, from want of use, become stiff and brittle.

The influence of fencing as an exercise to cure rheumatism and bring the limbs once more under the influence of the brain is very remarkable, and I have cured more than one case of incipient rheumatism by its means, while the immunity from accidents, falls, contusions, and sprains enjoyed by fencers needs no reiteration.

Fencing on the modern system, introduced by Ling, and modified by myself, is far superior as a means of physical education, to the old method in use in France. The difference comes from the attitudes used in each.

In the old school, when on guard, the left arm is raised, and the chest is flat. The result of long exercise in this posture, is to make a round-backed high-shouldered man. The modern system employs a different attitude. The left arm is down, the forearm and back of the hand behind the back, which is hollowed, the chest being arched outwards. I have consulted on this subject several eminent physicians, who have been my pupils at different times, and they have all agreed that physiologically, the tendency of the modern system

Saber fencers drilling at Ling's Central Institute of Physical Culture.

of fencing must be far superior to the French system, as a means of physical education.

By experience, I find that twenty-five minutes a day in fencing, including a rest of five minutes between each assault of ten minutes, is the utmost exercise that is beneficial to the body, leaving the frame vigorous. The practice of fencing by boys, as contrasted with that of gymnastics on the German Turner system[3], tends to make a lad tall and slender. Turners are invariably short and thick-set, if they commence training early. I have heard thus doubted, and have been pointed to many tall members of the Turnverein, as a proof that heavy gymnastics do not stop the growth.

Whenever I have questioned these tall Turners, I have always found that they took up gymnastics at twenty-one, or beyond that age, after they had attained their full growth. I determined to experiment on this point with my own son, Thomas Emilio Monstery. I took him at twelve years old, in California, and trained him on my own system. He grew three inches and a half in the first year of training in fencing, boxing, and swimming. The first exercise was for culture, the others for service in time of need.

At the end of that time I was persuaded to allow him to join the Turnverein for a year, to give that system a fair trial. In that year he grew one inch and a half. I then took him back, and trained him myself for five more months, during which he grew one and three-quarters inches. At that time he left me and ran away to sea, where he lived the laborious life of a sailor before the mast. From that day he stopped growing entirely, and is today a short man. He became strong and muscular, and weighed, at nineteen, 160 lbs., but he lost his flexibility entirely till he resumed the practice of fencing.

This, and my experience with my other boys since Emilio, shows me that boys need varied exercise to develop them. Let them run, jump, swim, box, fence, and play, but never try any cast iron system for them. Even fencing must not be carried so far with them that they get sick of it. They must be interested in their exercises to gain any benefit from them, and the work must be varied, as in nature.

With full grown men, gymnastics for one year, on the Turner system, may benefit the man, if he has got his full growth, and cannot fence or box for lack of means to pay a teacher. If a good teacher is at hand, and the man has means to pay him, he will get most benefit from the exercises of chivalry.

For men of sedentary habits, and between thirty and forty years old, fencing lessons are the best form of exercise that can be devised, as far as my experience goes. I will give some instances from my pupils.

I met Judge Chittenden, of California, in 1860, when I was coming from Mexico. He was about forty-five, and white-headed already. He had to leave California every year for the Mexican Highlands, on account of nervous debility from overwork. He came to my academy in San Francisco, and took fencing lessons. In a year I cured him, and he stayed with me for five years, becoming a most powerful man, and the best fencer of all my pupils.

A. C. Whitcomb, a lawyer of Boston, was six feet one and a half inches high, but a regular threadpaper; his chest narrow, and most of his family dead of consumption. He came to my academy with his partner, Mr. Pringle, to fence, and stayed till his chest rounded, and he became a powerful, burly man, in perfect health. He is now, I believe, in Paris, and gives promise of long life.

I might give plenty of other instances from my record of pupils, lawyers, doctors, editors, invalids, cured by fencing, but the list would become tedious. I am ready to give such names, if any persons are desirous to know whether fencing would benefit their particular cases.

After fencing, for physical culture, I place boxing and swimming. If a person comes to me to learn fencing, I ask: "Can you box?" If he says "No," I tell him: "Then you must learn. It is a necessity, like swimming, for your protection in danger. If you have not means and time to practice all three exercises, take boxing first."

This I repeat for all gentlemen. Boxing is the first necessity for a gentleman, unless he wishes to be imposed upon whenever he comes into the company of rough men, stronger than himself. It is necessary, if he wishes to be able to protect a lady from insult, a position in which a man often finds himself. If fencing is for physical culture, boxing is for use in life, and to avoid the temptation to take life by shooting.

Therefore, in the articles which follow, I shall begin with boxing and follow with fencing; for whereas there are many modes or exercise, such as calisthenics, that may be used instead of fencing by persons unable to afford the expense of fencing lessons, nothing can supersede boxing for use. I believe firmly in all the chivalrous arts, first among which I place boxing.

There are many secrets in this art which are not known to the rough prizefighters, first among which is the art of striking. I teach no rough characters these secrets, for they would make a bad use of them. I keep them for the protection of the decent and honorable members of society, and for no one else; so that if one of my pupils finds himself insulted in the street, or forced into a fight by a ruffian, he may know how to put in a single blow which shall take the fight out of the ruffian without injuring the knuckles of the striker. I have found that my pupils, small or large, knowing by experience what a terrible power they possess, are, as a rule, peaceable and quiet.

Finally, I say fence for physical cultivation, box for practice. Follow nature in your living. Don't eat too much, but eat enough. Avoid dieting, and exercise in the open air when you can. If you cannot get into the air a tonic may be necessary, for the strength must be kept up. I have found sometimes that weak whiskey and water helps me when I run down in the summer from confinement, but nothing will do such good as a change of air and a hunting expedition.

So, having said my say, we can afford to begin next week with the first of chivalrous arts—boxing.

Endnotes

1 Pehr Henrik Ling (1776–1839) was fencing master at the Central Institute of Physical Culture in Stockholm, and a noted pioneer of gymnastics, therapeutics, and physical culture.

2 Monstery possibly alludes to an incident that took place about 1839, when an ailing Ling rose from his sickbed to lecture, for the last time, at the Artillery Academy at Marieberg. There, after being interrupted by two disrespectful young officers, Ling ordered the two to take up their swords. "Ling, on the occasion, held a foil in each hand, and in one sally disarmed both the young and very skillful swordsmen." See Augustus Georgii, *A Biographical Sketch of the Swedish Poet and Gymnasiarch Peter Henry Ling* (London: H. Bailliere, 1854), 36–37.

3 A system of gymnastics and physical development begun in 1811 by the Prussian nationalist Friedrich Ludwig Jahn (1778–1852). The Turner system quickly spread to the United States, where *Turnvereins*, or German gymnastic clubs, began springing up in the major cities.

II.

THE LOGIC *of* BOXING.

First among the chivalrous arts, which every gentleman should know, I place the art of boxing. I place it there without hesitation, because I hold that every gentleman should be able to protect himself from insult and violence, with or without weapons. You call yourself, for example, a gentleman, and fancy that you are superior to the laborer, the hack-driver, the butcher, and cartman. You have more money than they, and more intellect. Yet, when the time comes that you are matched physically, the rough man is your superior, and you must yield to him. This should not be. A gentleman ought to be superior to a laborer physically as well as mentally, and especially should he be at all times superior to a rowdy. The rowdy is a mere wild beast that has strength and practice in natural rough-and-tumble fights, and yet a gentleman, if he knows the way, has the advantage over such a ruffian. I say to all gentlemen that your advantages are three over the ruffian: First, you have a flexible body, not stiffened by labor, but capable of being trained to anything; second, you have an intellect that will make you the superior in a contest that requires subtlety; third, you have means to pay for the best teachers, while the rowdy must teach himself, and nature does not teach how to strike a straight blow. Many gentlemen have said to me that they are not strong enough to give them any chance in such a fight. I have told them that it is not a matter of strength, but address, and especially of knowing how to strike a blow. A rowdy may be able to strike you ten times in a fight, and yet not hurt you severely, if you know how to parry and dodge, while, if you can get in a single blow, you may be able to take all the fight out of him at once. Therefore the first thing I teach my pupils is how to strike a really punishing blow. Any man can parry a blow after a fashion, but no man can strike a punishing blow by following nature. The natural boxer, like the natural swordsman, uses the *cut*, where the scientific boxer uses the more deadly *stab*, which shocks the nerve system of his opponent; and no man alive can stand more than three such full-arm blows as I teach my pupils to deliver. Were such blows delivered by professionals we should hear of no more prize-fights, for they would become too deadly. Not one boxer in the prize ring today understands the art of striking properly. It was the secret of the great success of Tom Sayers[1] that he knew how to strike. The Benicia Boy[2], with all his strength, never learned this art, and it was the cause of his failure. His hands were always used up before the end of a fight, because he injured his own knuckles as much or more than his enemy's hard skull.

I repeat that boxing is not a matter of strength as much as of art. It is the art of throwing all the strength you have into every blow, and of preserving your own hands from injury while injuring an opponent. I myself am a slender man, weighing only 134 lbs., and yet I have found, in my travels among the desperadoes of Mexico and Central America, that the worst ruffians were more afraid of my fist than of sword or knife. Another reason why I insist that gentlemen should learn to box is that it prevents that frequent use of deadly weapons, which is such a disgrace to our civilization. I have known many small, delicate men, with high spirit, who have been in the habit of carrying pistols for self-defense till I have taught them to box. After that they have always ceased carrying pistols, feeling a confidence that they could use the weapons of nature with sufficient force to protect themselves from the insults or outrages of ruffians stronger than themselves.

The above may be called the logic of boxing, the reasons why a gentleman should learn it. We will now go to its practice.

First Lesson in Boxing—On Balance and Striking.

All the exercises of chivalry are started from the "position of a soldier," as prescribed by military tactics. The pupil will assume this position at the command—

Attention!

Heels on a line and together, feet turned out at an angle of sixty degrees, knees straight without stiffness, body erect on the hips, inclining a little forward, arms hanging naturally, elbows near the body, palms of the hands to the side, little finger on the seam of the pantaloons, head erect, to the front, chin drawn in, eyes front.

The instructor commands—

1. For Boxing. 2. Position.

At the word "Position," the pupil turns slightly to the right, making a pivot of the left heel, and steps back with the right foot, from twelve to eighteen inches, according to height, keeping both shoulders square to the front, the feet at right angles, the left foot pointing to the front, the heels on a line, the weight of the body on the right hip, the left foot placed lightly, so that it can be drawn back in case of a kick made at it. The body must be erect, and the whole position solid and balanced on the right hip, so that the body can be leaned forward suddenly to strike out with violence, without losing the equilibrium. The legs are to be kept straight, and not bent as in fencing.

Front!

At this command the pupil resumes position of a soldier. The instructor will now correct his faults by example, and will practice him with the command "Position!" "Front!"—"Position!" "Front!" as many times as necessary, till the pupil executes the changes promptly and with decision. He will close with "front," and allow the pupil to rest. The exercise will be resumed at the command—

Guard![3]

At this command the pupil takes boxing position as described above. In addition to position of the legs he now learns position of arms.

Bring the left elbow to the side, the forearm nearly horizontal, but rather below than above the line of the elbow, the centre of the forearm on left hip, back of the hand oblique, thumb above fingers closed on the palm of the hand, the thumb closed between the second

and third joints of the second finger, the wrist straight. The straight line from the elbow along the back of the hand to the first knuckle of the middle finger is called the "line of power."[4]

Bring the right elbow in front of the pit of the stomach (called by boxers "the mark"), the forearm diagonal, hand to the left of and about four inches in front of the chin, clenched the same as the left, wrist straight. (See figure left.) The instructor now gives the command—

Spar![5]

Guard!

The pupil will alternately lift and plant the left foot lightly, the toe on the floor. As the foot rises, draw back left hand and advance right hand; as it falls, advance left hand and draw back right, these being the motions of striking and guarding. They must be kept going all the time, so that the muscles may be ready to execute any desired motion, without starting from a rest. They must be made lightly, saving the power for effective motions. The position of a soldier is resumed at the command—

Front!

The instructor commands, *Guard—Spar—Front! Guard—Spar—Front!* as often as he thinks necessary, till the pupil changes position rapidly, spars easily, and keeps his weight on the right leg, prepared for any movement. Then, being at guard, the instructor gives the word—

Advance!

The pupil doubles the distance between the feet by stepping forward with the left foot, and follows with the right. After due practice of this the instructor next commands—

Retreat!

The pupil doubles the distance between the feet by stepping back with the right, following with the left. The instructor practices the advance and retreat till it is performed with ease, when he commands—

Double—Advance!

At the word, *Advance*, the pupil makes two quick steps forward with the left foot, following with the right, being especially careful not to diminish the distance between the feet from that presented at Guard.

Double—Retreat!

At the word, *Retreat*, the pupil steps back quickly twice with the right foot, following with the left, as in the advance, and preserving same distance between the feet. The next command is—

At Will—Advance!

The pupil advances with a series of short, quick, steps, the length of the room, till the word—*Halt! At Will—Retreat!*

The pupil retreats in the same manner. The advance and retreat must be practiced till they become easy and rapid, the guard being carefully preserved all the time, and the sparring kept up at every step. A rest will be taken at the word—*Halt!* The instructor will now explain the next exercise, which is performed at the command—

Rear—Leap!

Leap to the rear with both feet simultaneously, and in the leap strike the left heel smartly against the right, coming down with the feet apart at the distance of Boxing Position or Guard. This leap is very important and must be practiced frequently, as it enables you to escape a blow that you cannot parry, and leaves you on guard against an enemy who must throw himself open to follow you. There is no front leap. One does not leap into danger, but out of it.

The first lesson will close with the practice of striking, which will be executed by the following orders from the position of Guard:

1. Take—2. Striking—3. Position!

At the word, *Position*, the pupil drops both hands, so that the wrists rest on the hips (see figure opposite), elbows drawn in, the line of power directed toward the object aimed at, the backs of the hands down, thumbs above, shoulders square to the front, upper part of

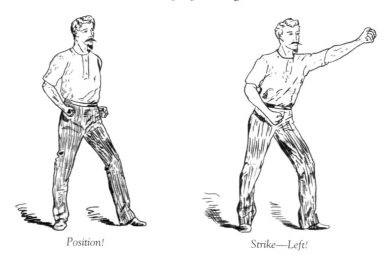

Position!   *Strike—Left!*

the body inclined forward, legs straight, the hips thrown back to counteract the force thrown forward in striking.

Ready!

The instructor next commands—

Strike—Left!

At the word, *Left,* the pupil strikes diagonally upward to the front with the left hand, advancing the left shoulder till the left fist and right shoulder are in a line, the left hand held obliquely from left to right.[6] The instructor stands in front and holds up the palm of his hand for the pupil to strike against, and lets it remain there, while he explains that the blow must proceed in the line of power from the elbow to the first centre knuckle of the hand, and must be struck with the whole surface of the four fingers, so as to keep the knuckles from being injured, as no single joint is strong enough to sustain the blow.

Strike—Right!

Strike—Right!

The left shoulder being in advance, the pupil now strikes up with the right hand in the same manner as the left, the left band being drawn back as the right advances, like the walking-beam of a steam engine, and being brought to rest again on the hip, shoulders again in a line. The position of the right hand will be oblique from right to left, exactly opposite to that of the left hand, and the close of each blow should leave the arm and hand in a straight line from the opposite shoulder to the middle of the object aimed at.

The instructor will continue this exercise by the words—*Left—Right—Left—Right!* correcting the pupil's faults of striking, and observing that the blow must follow the line of power at all times, never rising above it, in which case it becomes a cut, but preserving the diagonal direction which makes it a stab.

The pupil will now repeat these lessons at home, and will practice the striking lessons before a looking glass till they are perfectly performed, by striking at his own image in the glass, observing always to strike at the centre of the face. It must not be thought that blows in an actual set-to[7] are delivered in this manner. These are called "full arm" blows, and in a set-to occupy too much time to deliver. It is, however, necessary to learn them, in order to make the subsequent half arm blows really effective.

Endnotes

1 Tom Sayers (1826–1865), an English bare-knuckle boxing champion, was known as the "Little Wonder" and "Napoleon" of the Prize Ring. During his eleven-year career he lost only one of sixteen matches.

2 John Camel Heenan (1834–1873), an American bare-knuckle champion, was born in West Troy, New York. He was best known for his fight against Sayers, which ended in a draw when riotous spectators overran the ring.

3 The guard "is the position best calculated for attack and defence, and is that which a sparrer assumes in front of an antagonist." L. Hillebrand, *Sparring: Or, The Theory and Practice of the Art of Self Defence* (Philadelphia: Fisher & Brothers, 1864), 16.

4 In an 1887 interview, Monstery defined the line of power as proceeding "from the shoulder to the knuckles of the second, third and forefingers." *Macon Telegraph*, Jan. 6, 1887.

5 "The correct definition of the word Boxing is striking with the fist. That of Sparring is the practice for improving the art. This term is also applied to those habitual motions of the arms during a contest, while watching an opportunity to strike." Hillebrand, *Sparring*, 17. Also, to spar is defined thus: "To make the motions of attack and defense with the arms and closed fists; use the hands in or as if in boxing, either with or without boxing-gloves; practise boxing." William Dwight Whitney, ed., *The Century Dictionary and Cyclopedia*, vol. 7 (New York: The Century Co, 1897), 5795.

6 Monstery further clarified his striking technique in a later exchange published in *The Spirit of the Times*: "A dispute has arisen between certain of your readers in regard to Prof. Monstery's instruction in boxing, which is not quite plain enough to be understood by all. A bets that at the finish of a blow struck by the left, a line drawn from the left fist to the left shoulder and thence through the chest to the right shoulder should be straight, and when struck with the right, the line from that fist to left shoulder should be straight. B bets that when striking with the left hand, the right shoulder should be thrown forward so as to strike diagonally across the body, and when striking with the right the left shoulder should be thrown forward

in the same way. Which is right, or are both wrong? *Answer.*—A is right. The line should be perfectly straight to make a perfect blow, reaching as far forward as the conformation of the striker will permit. Blows should always be struck at the dummy in this way, and in a fight if you get a good chance. B loses the bet." *The Spirit of the Times,* Feb. 9, 1878.

7 "A set-to is a sparring contest between two opponents, and is generally divided into short combats called rounds, with periods of rest between." Hillebrand, *Sparring,* 17.

III.

STANDING *and* STRIKING.

The learner has found out in the first lesson how to balance his body, how to assume the proper position from which to strike out effectively, how to advance and retreat without breaking his guard, how to leap out of danger while keeping ready to strike, and how to strike the full arm blow from the hip with each hand alternately, without attending to the guard.

The second lesson teaches him how to strike with each hand from the position of "guard" high or low, at a figure representing an antagonist, and which offers resistance to the blow, compelling it to be delivered properly to avoid injury to the hand.

For this lesson a dummy should be provided, made of a hard stuffed bolster fastened against a wall or post. A bag of oats leaning against the wall of a barn, and rested on a bench or chair, will do, but it must not be suspended like the bag ordinarily used in training, so as to swing freely. It is essential that the dummy should offer resistance to the blow, and it should be as long as the body of a man and raised on a support as high as the legs of a man, to simulate the real body struck against in actual boxing. It must not be too soft either, or the pupil will be able to strike carelessly.

Blows are divided into "full-arm" and "half-arm" blows. Full arm blows are made from the wrist resting on the hip; half-arm blows are made from the elbow resting on the hip, or any position further forward. Blows are made high and low. High blows are directed at the centre of the face of the antagonist, low blows at "the mark." High blows are to be preferred, as they do not uncover the body; low blows are dangerous, as they expose the face to stopping-blows, but if one can be got in during a confused rally it generally decides a battle if it reaches "the mark." The instructor will stand before the dummy and show the pupil how to strike with the left. He then places the pupil before the dummy in position of "guard" and sparring, and commands—

1. Left—2. Aim—3. Strike!

At the word "Aim" the left wrist is rested on the left hip, the eyes fixed on the dummy. At the word "Strike!" the pupil executes the full-arm blow as in the first lesson, retaining his guard with the right arm (see figure below), leaving the hand resting on the dummy, which is struck with full force, leaving a straight line from the left fist to the right shoulder. The instructor corrects the position of the hand if necessary, and repeats the lesson till the left full-arm blow is properly delivered.

Strike—Left!

Strike—Left!

He then proceeds to teach the right-arm blow, which is much more difficult.

The "line of attack" is the perpendicular line which passes through the centre of the antagonist's body—in this instance the dummy. All blows must be delivered in this line or they lose their power and pass the enemy. In striking with the left, the boxer experiences no trouble, because the line of power of the left arm is already directed forward toward the enemy. The mirror lessons likewise offer the same advantage for both hands. In striking from position of "guard" the case is different, from the necessity of protecting the body by the use of the right arm, which is thrown across the body at an angle to the line of attack, to fend off the enemy's blows. It is first necessary, therefore, to bring this arm to the line of attack and to drop the hand from its guard position to make the line of power and the line of attack coincide. The instructor shows the pupil how to do this, places him before the dummy in "guard" position, and commands—

1. Right—2. Aim—3. Strike!

At the word "Aim," the pupil advances the left shoulder toward the dummy, and drops the right hand to a position where the forearm is horizontal from the elbow. It is now in the line of attack. At the word "Strike!" the full arm blow is delivered at the dummy, the left arm raised in guard. (See figure below). The instructor corrects the position of the hand as with the left, and observing that the straight line from the right hand to the left shoulder is preserved.

Strike—Right!

The pupil will now be exercised in striking high with left and right, by the above commands, till the blows are given correctly and with full force, without injury to the knuckles.

Strike—Right!

The instructor then commands—

1. Left and Right—2. At Will—3. Strike!
1. Right and Left—2. At Will—3. Strike!

Which are executed rapidly without the numbers and without the guard, but as in first lesson, till done with ease, when they will be found an excellent physical exercise.

The instructor will next explain the mechanism of half-arm blows. They are dealt in the same manner as full arm blows, but from a position nearer to the enemy, the elbow instead of the wrist being on the hip, or even further forward. They are executed by the commands—

1. Left—2. Half-arm—3. Strike!
1. Right—2. Half-arm—3. Strike!

These blows require no further explanation. They are weaker modifications of the full arm blow, but are the only attacking blows possible in a sparring match between skillful boxers, except in countering, inasmuch as full arm blows take too much time to avoid being stopped. Half-arm blows should be practiced frequently against the dummy for this reason, and for their use in a rally when they can be rapidly delivered.

The instructor now teaches the low blows from the standing position. He first explains the method of delivering them by his own example, then places the pupil before the dummy, and commands—

1. Strike low—2. Left—3. Aim—4. Strike!

At the word "Aim," draw the left shoulder up and backward, the hand opposite the left breast, the centre of the forearm above the nipple, back of the hand to the left. This places the arm in the line of power downward. At the word "strike," deliver the blow diagonally downward on the dummy, at the height of your own mark, the back of the hand up. It is necessary to make this blow something of a push to produce the all effect, and, as it strikes on a soft place in the enemy's body, the knuckles will not be injured. The guard must be maintained during the blow. The instructor then commands, after a similar explanation—

1. Strike low—2. Right—3. Aim—4. Strike!

At the word "Aim," the pupil throws the left shoulder forward and throws up the right shoulder and forearm, delivering the blow at the command "Strike" the same as with the left hand. In both these blows the guard must be kept with the non-striking hand. The instructor now cautions the pupil to practice these lessons at home on a dummy, or if that cannot be procured, before a mirror, and this terminates the second lesson.

IV.

ADVANCING *to* STRIKE
and FEINTING.

In the second lesson of boxing the pupil has been taught to strike from a standing position within distance of the dummy. He will now come one degree nearer to the conditions of actual contest. A skillful boxer never commences a battle with an antagonist within such a distance that the latter can strike him without moving his feet. He always begins out of distance, and uses the "advance," in order to get in on his opponent. The natural boxer is herein at a disadvantage, as he generally walks forward, thereby giving warning to the assault, instead of using the advance. The skillful boxer keeps sparring out of distance and watching his opportunity to slip in his left foot without observation, so that he can follow it up with an unexpected blow from within the proper distance. In order to learn the way to do this it must be practiced before the dummy, which will be found very useful in the progress of the whole course of lessons.

The third lesson commences with advancing and striking in four different ways; that is, with either hand, high and low.

The instructor places the pupil at such a distance from the dummy that he must step in to reach it, and, after showing the pupil how to execute the lesson, commands—

By count—Advance and strike left high—One! Two!

At the word "One" the pupil doubles the distance between the feet by stepping forward with the left, the left wrist going back as in the sparring motion. At the word "Two" he brings up the right foot and makes the blow at the dummy with the left hand, simultaneously with the planting of the right foot.

The instructor next commands—

By count—Advance and strike right high—One! Two!

At the word "One," the left foot is advanced with the left shoulder, the right arm being sunk to the position of "Strike Right." At the word "Two," the right foot follows, and the right arm blow is delivered simultaneously with the planting of the right foot.

The instructor then commands successively:

By count—Advance and strike left low—One! Two!

Also,

By count—Advance and strike right low—One! Two!

These are executed in the same manner as the high blows, with the difference of the position of arms and direction of blow. The instructor is careful to show, by precept and example, that the object of the first movement in each case is merely to bring the body into the same position as that from which the blows are delivered in the first dummy lesson. He is also careful to correct the common fault of the pupil of striking out too soon, or before the light foot is planted, in which case the blow is out of distance, spent, weak, and inefficacious. The four blows being thoroughly learned by the count, the instructor places the pupil at double distance from dummy, and commands successively:

By count—Double advance and strike left high—One! Two! Three!
By count—Double advance and strike right high—One! Two! Three!
By count—Double advance and strike left low—One! Two! Three!
By count—Double advance and strike right low—One! Two! Three!

At the words "One" and "Two" the distance is gained; at the word "Three" the blow is delivered, as the right foot touches the ground. Single and double advance and strike will be practiced till they are perfectly executed.

The distance from the dummy is now increased again.

The instructor next commands successively:

At will—Advance and strike left high!
At will—Advance and strike right high!
At will—Advance and strike left low!
At will—Advance and strike right low!

The pupil in each case advances and strikes on the same principles as before, the instructor warning him to keep sparring at every step of the advance, and to be careful not to strike till the right foot is firmly planted within distance.

The pupil is now ready to go to the next branch of the lesson.

FEINTS[1]

The instructor explains the first feint, and commands, when the pupil is out of distance:

1. Feint—Left high! 2. Prepare left! 3. Strike left!

At the first command the pupil strikes left high, still out of distance; at the second he brings back the left hand to the hip; at the third command he steps in and strikes left high at the dummy.

The instructor next commands successively:

Feint—Left high, and strike low! One! Two! Three!
Feint—Left low, and strike high! One! Two! Three!

The motions are executed at the call of the count, in the same manner as the first feint, only varying in direction of the blow as finally delivered. The left hand is the only one used in feinting. The feint with the right is too dangerous, as it takes away the guarding hand. The above are also the only feints capable of use in the attack, but both hands are used in countering, as will be explained in a later lesson, and they will, therefore, be now practiced on the dummy, to secure ease of motion.

These motions are not for use in the attack on a skillful adversary, but to be practiced when an opening occurs. They are as follows:

> Feint left and strike right high.
> Feint left and strike right low.
> Feint right and strike left high.
> Feint right and strike left low.

In each case the count will be, "One! Two!" At "one" the first blow is delivered out of distance, the opposite arm being prepared; at "two" the shoulder is reversed, the left foot planted, the right advanced, and the blow delivered with the opposite hand as the foot touches the ground, the guard being preserved all through.

This closes the dummy lessons, but the pupil who wishes to become a good boxer should practice them constantly during his succeeding course, for the benefit of health and skill.

The next lesson treats of the parries.

Endnotes

1 A strike made from out of distance, intended to draw a reaction from the antagonist.

V.

SIMPLE PARRIES *in* BOXING.

Parries[1] in boxing are divided into perfect and imperfect. With the imperfect we have nothing to do. They are all those parries where the arm is exposed to injury by meeting a blow with the side of the wrist at right angles to the coming shock. They may fend off a blow, but if the boxer is figuring with a man of superior strength, he may yet sustain serious injury through the crippling of his arms.

Perfect parries are those which strike off a blow without exposing the delicate bones of the arm to injury.

There are six simple parries, namely: Right and left, high and low, outside, and right and left high, inside. The inside parries are only used in the rally, when both parties are fighting within distance.

To commence the parries it is best for the instructor to put on the boxing gloves with the pupil, in order to avoid injury if the latter is clumsy, but if he be intelligent, the gloves can be dispensed with during the school of the simple parries.

The first taught is:

Right Hand Parry.

The instructor directs the pupil to observe that, as they stand opposite, in the position of guard, the right side of the face is open to attack from the opponent's left hand, which is foremost. He directs the pupil to strike left high at the instructor's face, which the instructor parries with the right. Having shown the pupil the way, he tells him to parry, the instructor striking with the left hand high at the pupil's face.

The pupil being in guard position, and sparring, sees the blow coming. He strikes out with the right hand diagonally upward, forward, and to the right, passing his own face with right forearm, meeting the opponent's wrist with the strong cushion of muscle and the hard tendon on the outside of the right fore arm, striking off the blow with violence, the hand above the opponent's head, unless he is much taller than the one who parries, so that the opponent is seen inside the right arm.

Right Hand Parry

The next is:

Left High Parry.

This parry is used against the attack of the opponent's right hand, high. It differs from the right high parry, inasmuch as it starts from a different position. Whereas the right hand is already in a line oblique to the enemy's line of attack, and only needs to be struck out to divert the blow; the left hand is in the same line as the coming attack, and must be brought oblique thereto before the blow can be perfectly parried. If the left be simply struck up, like the right hand, it may miss the blow or go outside thereof. Moreover, if the enemy's blow be a round hand blow, the bend of his right arm may pass the parry, rendering it inefficacious, for it must be remembered that the right-hand blow of a natural boxer is almost always delivered with the elbow to the right, so as to come in a curved line.

The instructor directs the pupil to strike at him with the right hand high, and parries with left high parry, till the pupil has learned it. Then he tells the pupil to parry, and strikes at him in turn with the right hand high.

The pupil, seeing the blow coming, brings the left hand into line obliquely across the body, and throws up the arm in a right angle over the head, the elbow as high as the ear, back of the hand up, crossing the opponent's wrist with the outside of the left forearm, and following the blow.

This parry is peculiarly effective against a round hand blow with the

Left High Parry

right, as it catches the hand of the striker on the upper elbow of the parrier, sometimes breaking the wrist, as recently happened to Mr. Stephen Taylor[2], in a glove contest with Prof. Miller[3], the Graeco-Roman wrestler.

Next follows:

RIGHT LOW PARRY.

This is very simple, and made from any position of the arm, high or low, the blow being struck diagonally down and outward, smartly and decidedly.

Right Low Parry

The last outside parry is:

LEFT LOW PARRY.

This is executed with the left hand, in the same manner. In each case the arm is straightened, and brought into the line of defense, and the parry made with the inside of the arm, striking the opponent's wrist with the heel of the hand, or the open palm, as sharply as possible.

These are all the parries made from the position of guard against a common attack, high or low. The other two are called "inside parries," and are only used during a rally when the blows are already at half-arm distance.

They are:

LEFT INSIDE—AND RIGHT INSIDE—PARRY.

To teach them the instructor makes the pupil strike at him right and left high, in quick succession, directing him to leave his hands there.

Left Inside Parry   *Right Inside Parry*

The instructor parries the blows, thus, leaving the arms up, the opponent's arms outside. The opponent then withdraws one of his hands and strikes half-arm blows inside the guard.

The parrier, his arms being up, shifts the elbow and hand across the face, parrying the blows with the elbow and forearm, moved so far to the right or left that the opponent can be seen outside of the guard, just as in the outside parries he can be seen inside the guard.

These inside parries terminate the simple parries of the fourth lesson. The fifth lesson is occupied with effective or counter parries.

Endnotes

1 "Parrying is beating a blow out of its line, with the hand or arm, to make it miss the point aimed at." Hillebrand, *Sparring*, 16.

2 An article published during the period noted that William Miller "boxed Steve Taylor at Billy Edwards' benefit, in Turner Hall; broke Taylor's arm and bested him." *Cincinatti Daily Times*, Aug. 26, 1876.

3 The great Graeco-Roman wrestling champion William Miller (1846–1939). Born in England and raised in Australia, Miller instructed in San Francisco, New York, and Baltimore from 1874 onward, and in addition to wrestling, held championships in boxing, fencing, weight lifting, and long distance walking. During the 1870s, Miller assisted Monstery in a number of fencing and sparring exhibitions, and, notably, served as Monstery's second in the 1876 fencing contest between Monstery and Senac.

VI.

PARRIES *with* RETURNS.

The simple parries given in the previous lesson would, of course, be deprived of half their value were they used only as a means of escaping from the opponent's blow without enabling the pupil to make an offensive return.[1] They will, therefore, be combined with returns, and these parries and returns should be frequently practiced with the master, or with fellow pupils in the school, not in the form of a set-to, but as a practice for the benefit of eye and muscle; as quickness of return is an essential feature of skill in the art of boxing. The parries with returns are as follows:

1. RIGHT PARRY AND RETURN LEFT HIGH.
(TWO MOTIONS.)

(1.) When opponent leads left, execute "Right parry," bringing left hand to hip. (2.) Strike left high, bringing right hand on guard, as in the striking figure in the picture, to cover from opponent's return.

Right Parry and Return Left High

2. Right Parry and Return Left Low.
(two motions.)

(1.) Same as in previous exercise, but end with left hand at height of breast. (2.) Strike left low at opponent's "mark" covered.

3. Right Parry and Counter Left.
(one motion.)

When opponent leads left, lead with your own left covered, throwing right forearm across the face at height of the nose to guard against his blow. This is also called a "stopping blow," if given so as to anticipate opponent's blow.

4. Right Parry and Counter Left and Right.
(two motions.)

(1.) Same as before, but after counter prepare right. (2.) Step in and strike right, or you will find yourself out of distance, as your opponent will probably retire after his blow proves unsuccessful.

5. Right and Left Parry and Return Right.
(two motions.)

(1.) When opponent strikes left and right with great rapidity, parry both blows, and bring right hand to hip. (2.) Strike right.

6. PARRY RIGHT AND LEFT, AND RETURN RIGHT AND LEFT. (THREE MOTIONS.)

(1.) Same as previous exercise. (2.) Same, and prepare left. (3.) Step in and strike left, or you will be out of distance, as before explained.

If two pupils will carefully practice these exercises for a week, beginning slowly, and being careful always to strike according to rule, they will find their increase in rapidity and skill very marked, and will already be able to give a very creditable sparring exhibition.

These lessons comprise the whole art of boxing as formerly taught. The rest of the lessons are those first introduced by myself.

Endnote

1 "The Return Blow is one which is generally struck immediately after a parry." Hillebrand, *Sparring*, 16.

VII.

EFFECTIVE *or* COUNTER PARRIES
in BOXING.

The parries which I have shown in the previous lesson are all simple parries, so-called. They throw off the danger, but do not place the antagonist in any position of peril. The effective, or counter parries, are those which, besides warding off the antagonist's blow, expose him to your own blow in a position where he finds it difficult to parry. They are four in number:

1. PARRY AND RETURN RIGHT INSIDE
(THREE MOTIONS.)

The opponent leads left high. 1. Instead of beating off the blow by right parry (simple), which sustains the opponent, throw right hand and shoulder back with a sweep, the elbow forming a right angle, forearm perpendicular. 2. Level the forearm by a turn on the centre, raising the elbow and lowering the hand, bringing the forearm on a level directed toward the opponent's face, hand oblique. The line of power must be carefully observed, so that the blow will be taken by all the joints of the hand, or the second knuckles will suffer. 3. Deliver blow at opponent's face.

This parry is very effective against persons who lose their balance when striking by overreaching, also against those who disengage the arm too soon after a parry instead of following the arm (Left Inside

Parry). To avoid the counter herein described the pupil must remember, when delivering a blow, *never to leave the opponent's arm till out of his reach.*

2. Right Counter-Parry!

The pupil leads off with his left at the face. The instructor, instead of, as in Right Parry, meeting the blow, seeing the opponent inside the right arm, brings his hand down when struck at, executes a semicircle with the open hand under the opponent's arm, and wards off the blow with a smart push to his own left, thereby seeing his opponent outside of his own parry, and exposing him to a full-arm blow with the left. This parry throws the opponent off his guard and frequently brings his back toward you as in picture.

Right Counter-Parry!

3. Left Cross-Parry!

The pupil strikes left high as before. The instructor meets the opponent's hand with the open palm of the left hand, striking the blow down and to the right. This pulls the opponent toward you with his blow, destroying his guard, and laying him open to the full-arm blow of your right hand, frequently destroying his equilibrium.

Left Cross-Parry!

4. COUNTER CROSS-PARRY!

The pupil leads left high as before. The instructor, as the opponent strikes, inclines the body a little back, brings the left hand with a demi-circle under the opponent's left arm, and with a smart push forward and to the left, outside the opponent's arm, strikes off the blow downwards. This destroys the opponent's equilibrium and frequently brings his back to your right hand as in the picture.

This counter parry admits of no defense. One caught by it must duck his head and run.

Counter Cross-Parry!

VIII.

OFFENSE *and* DEFENSE *by* EVASIONS.

The defense from an enemy's blows by evasions I consider the most important part of the science of self-defense, though it ranks after offense in importance. I began to teach this part of boxing in 1853, and was at first ridiculed. In 1860 I introduced it in the Olympic Club in California[1], and while it was admitted that evasions constituted a perfect defense, it was thought that they could only be used by a person of great activity and skill, and were useless in common boxing lessons, as incapable of being taught. Since I demonstrated that they could be successfully taught to ordinary pupils, the practice of evasions has spread to a great extent; but they are commonly practiced in a ridiculous and unscientific manner, merely to escape from an adversary's blows, without securing any advantage. True and scientific evasions are very different from the dodgings and duckings that go under that name at many sparring exhibitions, where the body is simply drawn away from an opponent's blow, leaving him free to repeat it, and to escape the return. The advantages of a true evasion are double.

1st. It has been demonstrated that the head can be moved out of the line of an enemy's blow, after a little practice, faster than the blow can be sent, the distance traversed by the head being shorter than that which the hand is compelled to traverse.

2nd. If the blow can be escaped by an evasion, the party using the evasion has both hands free to strike, neither being occupied by parrying.

These advantages can only be gained by making the evasions side-wise, and toward the opponent, instead of backwards, as no advantage accrues unless the evasion brings you within striking distance of the opponent without danger to yourself. All evasions should be accompanied by counters or return blows. Evasions are divided into "Left" and "Right," and are as follows:

Left Evasions.

1. Left evasion, counter left.

(ONE MOTION.)

The opponent leads with the left. (Strike left at opponent as he leads, drawing in the back so as to bring the head to the left, escaping his blow, shoulders on a line with the blow).

2. Left evasion, counter right high.

(ONE TIME AND TWO MOTIONS.)

(1.) Draw in back and bring head to left as before, advancing the shoulder, but not striking left. At same time prepare right. (2.) Strike right outside your opponent's left arm. Practice this till you can join two motions in one, as this is a difficult evasion.

3. Left evasion, counter right and left high.

(TWO MOTIONS.)

(1.) Same as in second evasion, delivering right with opponent's blow, and prepare left. (2.) Strike left high.

4. Left evasion—counter left and right.
(TWO MOTIONS.)

(1.) Same as in first evasion, and prepare right. (2.) Strike right.

5. Left evasion—counter left high and right low.
(TWO MOTIONS.)

(1.) As in fourth evasion, but prepare right for low blow. (2.) Strike right low at opponent's left side—a dangerous blow, if delivered near the waist.

RIGHT EVASIONS.

1. Right evasion, and counter left high.
(ONE MOTION.)

Against opponent's left. (Strike left, inside of opponent's arm, throwing the left shoulder forward, head and body forward and to the right, as the blow comes.) Both shoulders will now be on a line with blow.

2. Right evasion, and counter right high.
(TWO MOTIONS.)

(1.) Right evasion as before, but advance the left shoulder, without striking left, and prepare right. (2.) Strike right, outside opponent's arm.

3. Right evasion, and counter left and right.
(TWO MOTIONS.)

(1.) As in first right evasion, strike left, and prepare right. (2.) Strike right.

4. Right evasion, and counter right and left.
(THREE MOTIONS.)

(1.) Same as in second right evasion. (2.) Same, and prepare left.
(3.) Strike left high.

5. Right evasion, and counter left high and right low.
(TWO MOTIONS.)

(1.) As in first right evasion, but also prepare right low. (2.) Strike
right low at opponent's left side, about waist.

DOUBLE EVASION.

This evasion is the most difficult to learn, but the most effective when
learned. The ducking, so common in sparring exhibitions, somewhat
resembles it, but fails in the important point that it provides for no
return at the adversary. This evasion is used against an opponent who
comes in, left and right, one after the other, viciously. It is executed
in the school by the commands—

Left and right evasion, and counter left and right.
(THREE MOTIONS.)

(1.) Deliver left, with left evasion of opponent's left hand. He strikes
back with his right at you.

(2.) Bring your head under opponent's left arm, with right evasion,
by a ducking motion, and prepare right. (3.) Step in and strike right,
or you will be out of distance.

This is a very fine motion for practice, especially after left evasion,
when you see opponent ready to strike right. By escaping this blow,
in the manner above set forth, you find yourself outside your oppo-

nent's guard, and he can hardly escape your right hand, which takes him by surprise. These evasions, like parries with returns, should be practiced frequently with a friend, according to the school, to secure quickness and readiness.

Endnote

1 The San Francisco Olympic Club, organized with Monstery's help in 1860, was located on Sutter Street between Montgomery and Sansome streets. Monstery's fencing academy was located nearby at 522 Montgomery Street.

IX.

TRIPS, GRIPS, *and* BACK-FALLS.

I teach the following tricks, not with any idea that they are to be used in friendly encounters with the gloves, but solely for the protection of gentlemen who may, at any time, against their will, be forced into an encounter with a street ruffian. They are in such a case exceedingly useful as, if executed by surprise, either of them may take all the fight out of an opponent at once. There are many of such tricks, of which I give only the most useful and effective, also the defenses against the same, if practiced on you by others. Remember that these are strictly surprises, only to be attempted when opportunity offers. The tricks are composed of evasions and front and rear changes. Before explaining them it will be necessary to speak of the changes.

"Front change" is executed by stepping to the front with the right foot from position of "Guard," wheeling on the left heel. This brings the right foot foremost, and the position of the arms should be reversed accordingly. At this stage of proficiency the pupil should practice this change so as to accustom himself to fight with either foot foremost.

"Rear change" is executed by stepping to the rear with the left foot, wheeling on the right heel. It is used in defensive motions, and leaves the right foot out as in front change.

In this chapter I treat of two back falls and of "head-locks," more generally known as "chancery" positions, which, however, I do not endorse as very dangerous to a skillful boxer, nor very advantageous to the user. The tricks are as follows:

1. Right Evasion, with Front Change Trip and Grip.

This trick is executed in three motions, if the opponent leads left. It is best done by previously drawing him on, and executing right parry, retreating once or twice. It is executed as follows:

(1.) Use right evasion and counter left at opponent's throat, leaving hand there. (2.) Instead of retreating, execute front change on left heel, throwing right hand forward so as to clutch opponent's right shoulder from the rear. The wheel brings your right knee behind the opponent's left knee. (3.) Press simultaneously with both hands and right knee quickly and suddenly, and you will throw your opponent on his back with a heavy fall.

[NOTE: Against a right-handed boxer, execute this on inverse principles, substituting "left" for "right," and *vice versa*, wherever it occurs.]

The defense against this fall is simple. Execute a front change simultaneously with your opponent, which saves your right shoulder from his grip. Then push him off, or strike right or left.

[NOTE: This throw can also be executed after a counter-cross-parry if your opponent hangs back, so that you do not succeed in throwing him off his balance, and delivering a good blow. The motions in this case are also three. (1.) Counter-cross-parry. (2.) Front change. (3.) Throw. If he hangs back still more, and retreats, the motions are four. (1.) Counter cross-parry. (2.) Step in with the left. (3.) Front change. (4.) Throw.]

2. BACK FALL, WITH TRIP AND GRIP.

This is also against opponent's left, and in two motions, as follows:

(1.) Execute right parry, and step forward with left foot, throwing weight on left leg (2.) Encircle the left leg of your opponent with your own right leg by a quick throw outside, and with both hands push suddenly at his chest or throat, holding on to his left leg with your own right, and throwing him on his back. This throw is one of the easiest to learn, and I have found it one of the most effective at the beginning of a fight, as it inflicts a very heavy fall. It can be attempted after any parry right or left. It is my own improvement over the ordinary back-fall taught. In old-fashioned boxing, where the right leg is thrown inside instead of outside. That fall can be escaped by throwing the leg around out of danger, but in the fall above described the leg of the opponent is instantly locked hard and fast. This fall is very effective against the threatened assault of a ruffian who stands close to you to bully you. It can be executed with the right foot forward by using the left leg for the trip, catching opponent's right leg if that is forward. The hand must push, and not clutch, or the opponent may catch at you to save himself.

The defense against this fall is either a rear change or a rear leap. Always be on your guard against it.

3. Head-Locks and Defenses.

There are two head-locks for each arm; front and rear.

The front head-lock is well known as "getting a man in chancery." It consists in catching him round the neck, and clutching his head under your arm, catching his outside wrist if possible, then punching away at his face.[1] Against an opponent much weaker than yourself, and very active, head-locks are effective, as keeping him within reach of punishment, but against one of equal or superior strength, they are very dangerous, as they expose the user to a heavy fall. If the man in chancery is stronger than his enemy, he can seize the punishing arm, and it becomes a mere wrestling struggle. If of nearly equal strength, he can seize opponent's leg, lift him, and throw him, falling on him.

*"Getting the head in chancery," illustrated in Edmund Price, **The Science of Self Defence**, 1867.*

It may be said that it is not allowed in the prize ring to seize the leg. I answer that I am not writing for or teaching prize-fighters. I am teaching gentlemen how to defend themselves if assaulted by ruffians, and how to take useful exercise with their friends with gloves on. In sparring head-locks are not allowed. In fighting a bully, if a gentleman gets caught in a front head-lock, I advise him: 1st. To keep his wrists from being seized. 2nd. To bury his face in his enemy's breast, taking the blows on the top of the head. 3rd. To grasp his enemy by the thigh with all his force, lifting him in the air so as to throw him. 4th. Failing that, to catch him by the waist and throw. 5th. Failing these, to get under the opponent, and lift him on the hip or back, so as to throw him over your head. All these are feasible defenses unless the enemy is twice as strong as you are, in which case I advise you to keep clear of his grip if possible. If, however, a stronger man than yourself gets you under his arm, and seizes your outside wrist, leaving you only one arm behind his back, there is still one way of escape. Throw the arm that is behind his back over his shoulder, so as to bring the hand in front of his throat, and press with your fingers on his windpipe, seeking for the "Adam's apple." The pain will compel him to let go, and his head will go back, leaving you in a position to give him a terrible back-fall, as you have your knee behind his.

The rear head-lock is much more dangerous than the other, and is thus executed: If you lead, and your antagonist uses an evasion, so that you find your arm over his shoulder, throw it instantly back round his neck, throw the weight of your body on him, and then grasp your own wrist with the other hand, trying to lift him from the ground, his whole weight on his neck, squeezing with all your might, so as to strangle him.[2]

The defenses against this lock are similar to the other. You can certainly seize his leg and try to lift him, and fall on him. Also you can feel up the line of his breast till you find the Adam's apple, and press on it, grasping him with the

The second "chancery" headlock, illustrated and described in Price's **The Science of Self Defence.**

other hand. When he yields, as he must, give the back fall. All must be done very quickly, or you will grow weak through suffocation.

As I have before said, I never advise head-locks, as they are too dangerous, if the opponent knows how to use his advantage.

Endnotes

1 A virtually identical technique, simply termed the first "chancery" position, is illustrated in Edmund Price's *The Science of Self Defence*, and is included here with Monstery's text. Price describes the technique thus: "You seize your adversary round the neck, with your left arm thrown over his right shoulder, which position brings you both facing the same way; having accomplished this, swing yourself round to the right, and stepping from your opponent at the same time with your right foot, bear him down by the neck till his head is on a level with your heart. Then either grasp your left wrist with your right hand and compress your hold with all your might: or if you think you can hold him tight with the left arm alone, do so and strike away at the unprotected face that presents itself to you." Edmund Price, *The Science of Self Defence. A Treatise on Sparring and Wrestling, Including Complete Instructions in Training and Physical Development. Also, Several Remarks Upon, and a Course Prescribed for the Reduction of Corpulency.* (New York: Dick & Fitzgerald Publishers, 1867), 81–82.

2 Again, a virtually identical technique, termed the second "chancery" head-lock, was illustrated by Edmund Price, and now accompanies Monstery's text. Price describes the technique thus: "At any time that I was at close quarters with an antagonist, and had led off with the left, which having missed its mark, and my left arm going over the left shoulder of my adversary, I would avail myself of that opportunity to throw it backwards round his neck, at the same moment throwing the whole weight of my body upon him, till I brought his head down to his left hip; then I would grasp my left arm at the wrist and lift my friend from the ground, making his head my fulcrum. Thus throwing the whole weight of my opponent upon his neck, which is the next thing to hanging a man." Price, *The Science of Self Defence*, 83–84.

X.

RULES *for a* SET-TO *with* GLOVES.

The school of boxing, already given, both in theory and practice, is designed to teach gentlemen how to defend themselves against assault, but it must not be supposed that it is sufficient to go through the school to become an expert boxer. That can only be attained by practice, and two friends can mutually assist each other by repeating the school at least once a week, and sparring at will at other times. In going through the school with each other, all blows should be struck in "certain time," that is, when your friend expects it. In a set-to with the gloves, on the other hand, all blows should be struck in "uncertain time," that is, after feints, and when he does not expect it. In order to make a set-to between friends useful, and at the same time agreeable, I have always enforced the following rules at my academy, whenever sparring takes place:

I absolutely prohibit—1. *Whipping;* 2. *Cutting;* 3. *Palming;* 4. *Round blows;* 5. *Trips and wrestling*, unless previously agreed on and practiced on soft ground.

I will describe these practices, and explain the reason for their prohibition to my pupils.

Whipping is executed with the end of the fingers after a blow has been parried, with a flirting motion of the wrist over the guard, so as to catch the opponent's face with the leather of the glove, and graze the skin. It is an abominable practice, only used by ill-natured and vicious sparrers, on purpose to hurt their fellow pupils. I have seen men's faces scratched severely in this way, especially where the whipper used the seam of the glove in their malicious play. If the same motion were used with the bare hand it would do no damage. In nine cases out of ten the fingers would not reach the face, and the wrist would be hurt in flirting over the guard, while the damage done would be a mere scratch. I, therefore, absolutely forbid whipping to my pupils.

Cutting is the common way of striking used by natural and unscientific boxers. If tried in a fight with the bare hands, it does not hurt like a true blow in the line of power, and it exposes the knuckles to injury in giving it. In glove sparring it is a malicious way of striking, as it forces aside the padding of the glove, and the blow comes with the edge of the hand, made harder by one fold of leather. Finally, cutting is too dangerous for a friendly set-to, and does not hurt nearly as much as a true blow, either in a glove fight or a real fight. Therefore, I forbid all cutting to my pupils.

Nevertheless, cutting is the most popular of all sorts of hitting in public sparring matches. A cut is a smart slap, and makes a loud noise, wherefore uninstructed audiences generally applaud a loud cut. A true blow, however heavy, makes no noise with the gloves, and is only noticed by its effects.

Palming is slapping with the open hand. In a bare-handed fight it is absurd. In a glove set-to it hurts severely, because the palm of a boxing-glove is not padded. I forbid it in my academy.

Round blows[1] are like cutting. In a fistfight they expose the knuckles to injury; in a glove set-to they force aside the padding and hurt severely. I forbid them entirely to my pupils.

Trips and wrestling are too dangerous to use in a friendly contest on a hard floor. For the sake of instruction, and when both sides agree to it, they may be practiced, but only on soft ground.

These are all the direct prohibitions. The general rules are simple. A set-to should be taken in a gentlemanly manner. Do not clench the fist tight, but strike with the back of the fingers, hand partly open, so that the fingers will yield to the blow. To clench the fist makes the blow harder, but no straighter, and a set-to should be conducted exactly the same as a fist fight, except that the fist should not be clenched. Thus conducted, it improves the boxer. Conducted with a view to hurt the opponent with the gloves, it leads to bad habits, makes a set-to disagreeable, and leads a man to trust to motions that would ensure his defeat with the naked fist.

The first rule of offense is never to strike a blow with the glove that you could not strike at a hard dummy with all your strength without injury to your hand. To convince yourself of the policy of this rule, try whipping, cutting, palming, and round blows with the naked fist against a hard wall or post with a thick blanket against it to save the skin from scratches. Deliver each with all your force and you will soon find their dangers, whereas you can strike a true blow without any bad consequences. This is the great reason I use dummy lessons for my pupils, to teach them how to balance the fist and avoid injury to wrist or knuckles. After long practice the knuckles are often grazed a little, but the injury is only skin deep, and can be avoided by using an old kid glove at first.

The first rule of defense is to watch your opponent's hands, not his eyes, as the old-fashioned boxers and fencers advised. A man cannot hit you with his eyes. The eyes indicate the moment of attack, but they never tell where the attack is coming. I have found it the best plan to fix the eyes on the centre of the opponent just below his chin, as then one can see his face and hands together.

Keep your guard according to the height of your opponent, and, in sparring with a man much taller than yourself, use evasions to defend yourself. If you parry and return you can seldom reach him.

Spar to the right by stepping to the right against a left-handed boxer, and spar to the left against a right-handed boxer. The object of sparring is to get outside his guard and find an opening.

Never attack in "certain time," but always with feints in "uncertain time," to deceive the opponent. After an attack, retreat straight back as quick as possible. In other words, hit and get away. Never retreat to the left from a left-handed boxer, or to the right from a right-handed one, as you come in the way of his opposite hand.

With a strange opponent, always find out his style before you attack. This is done by retreating so as to draw his blows. As counters are the most dangerous of all blows, avoid leading at a strange opponent, or you may meet his counter, either as a "stopper" or by evasions. By making him lead, you may get in your own counter, by evasion or otherwise. Against a heavy hitter, get away from his blows by retreat, and strike after him, as, if you parry his blows, their force may numb your arms.

These are all the rules I find it necessary to give to my pupils for sparring with each other. It may, however, happen, and often does, that they are induced to put on the gloves with strangers at other places, and that these try all sorts of unfair tricks on them, turning a friendly set-to into a glove-fight, all the more dangerous because no warning is given. This is very apt to be the case between the pupils of other teachers and my own, through a spirit of rivalry. I, therefore, subjoin special advice against the classes most dangerous to meet.

ADVICE AGAINST MALICIOUS BOXERS.

When you meet a *heavy hitter, who always cuts*, get away from his blow, and parry, if you must, with the elbow, as in left parry. Strike after him. If he "rushes" you, step to the right quickly, and, as he passes, strike right at the side of his head. Generally keep away till you see your chance to give him one good full-arm right-hander on the nose. That is the favorite blow of all my pupils against heavy men. Evasion of a cutter takes his blow on your shoulder, and if he is not too heavy, is recommended, as it gives you a heavy, full blow in return for a glancing shoulder cut. I have sickened a cutter before now, by setting my neck stiff, and meeting his hand with a butt, taking the blow on the thickest part of my skull, and dislocating his little finger. Against a round hitter, always parry with the elbow, as in "left parry," even if with the right arm. You catch his wrist with the strongest part of your own arm. If you lead with him, or before him, duck the head after your lead, and execute rear leap, and his blows will pass over your head.

Against whippers and palmers, go for close fighting, and watch your time for a right-hander. Against all malicious boxers, clench the fist, and wait your opportunity for one full-arm right or left hand blow. If your opponent is a heavy man who leads slowly, try to get in the "stopper" previously described.

Against a stranger, not malicious, but who is a right handed boxer, fighting with the right foot foremost, use left, parry and counter right or else use left evasion and counter left and right or right and left. Never use right evasion to a right-banded boxer. I also recommend counter-parry with the left hand, and counter-cross-parry with the right hand. Always keep the right hand well to the left of the chin, and spar to the left with such a boxer. These are all the rules I recommend for sparring.

ADVICE IN STREET ENCOUNTERS.

Always try to get in the first blow in a chance encounter. Parley with your enemy, and watch him till you see that you will be assaulted. Then give the first half-arm left-hand blow at his nerve system, and follow it with a full-arm right-hander at same place. I have generally found that I could finish such a battle in the one round.

If you are attacked first, remember that street ruffians almost always fight in "certain time." You can see the blow coming, and they depend on beating down your guard. Step to the right, and if your enemy rushes execute rear leap to the right, striking him as he passes. Remember that one or two right-hand blows at his nerve system, properly planted, finish a Hercules. Always follow any advantage with left and right, escape after a blow with rear leap. Never keep on fighting after receiving a severe blow, as you will get beaten if you do. Retreat till you have recovered from the shock. But always follow up an advantage.

The place to hit is for the *nerve system,* of which I have so often spoken. The best place is where the blow is most certain to reach the object, that is, in the centre of the opponent. In full face, strike for the nose; in profile, for the ear; when the back of the opponent is toward you, for the nape of the neck.

The blows which shock the nerve system by inflicting pain are: 1st, on the nose, especially if struck upwards or sidewise; 2nd, between the eyes; 3rd, on the mouth, cutting the lips on the teeth; 4th, on the side of the chin, jarring the brain; 5th, behind the ear; 6th, on the nape of the neck at the base of the skull.

The last two blows will stun an opponent. The last should be a cut like a hammer. It is seldom an opportunity is found to deliver it, except after a counter-cross-parry.

In a sudden difficulty with an impudent fellow, the straight back fall is almost certain to succeed. I have taken the fight out of more than one ruffian by its means.

My final advice on boxing is: Be civil to all, and never seek a quarrel, but if one is forced on you, strike quick and surprise your opponent.

Endnote

1 "Nearly all blows which are not delivered in a somewhat straightforward line, and which are commonly used by unskilled persons, are called round blows. They generally take effect upon the sides of the body or head, either with the fist or open hand." Hillebrand, *Sparring*, 87.

Col. Monstery's contribution this week is of a startling character. It describes rough-and-tumble fighting, its attacks and defenses, and considers not only the fist, but the head and the foot as weapons in combat. That style of fighting in Wales, where a man rushes at his enemy, leaps and strikes him with both feet in his face, is especially hideous, and we are willing to concede the Welsh a monopoly of it.

—*The Spirit of the Times*, March 9, 1878

XI.

OBSERVATIONS *on* NATURAL WEAPONS.

The first weapons of the gentleman are the same as those of any unarmed man—his hands. The savage has no idea of their capacities for anything but grasping and scratching, just as he has no idea of self-defense beyond the cumbrous expedient of the shield. The educated gentleman, who has trained his body as well as his mind, knows that he possesses three natural weapons, each of which is terrible in its way—his head, his fist, his foot. The only one of these which is thoroughly and instantly available at all times, with the minimum of danger to the user, is the fist, of the value of which I have endeavored, in the previous articles, to impart a knowledge to those persons who, being at a distance from my academy, are unable to learn of me personally. I do not wish it to be thought that I expect to make any man an accomplished boxer, simply by the perusal of my articles. There are many things in the art of boxing which can only be learned by actual practice with the master being as impossible to put into words as it is impossible to paint the effect of a flash of lightning. They are a series of positions instantly assumed, and each trick would require a dozen pictures to explain it, while the result would be unsatisfactory after all. What can be done by words and pictures I have done, giving the lessons much as I teach them, and those who are already natural or practical boxers can learn from these articles how to correct their style of hitting, but I cannot possibly give the benefit of my own criticism to a pupil who may misunderstand my words and require to be shown by example or corrected in his faults. Still, I can conscientiously say I am convinced that, if any man of good intelligence who has already sparred a little, practices the lessons I have laid down before the glass, or still better at a dummy, and studies especially the correct blows, the parries, and evasions, he will find it an immense advantage in any chance contest in which he falls with a natural fighter, such as frequent the street corners of every town and village in this country. Against a skillful boxer, he cannot expect to hold his own without constant practice, which I recommend him to take, but, if he ever comes to my academy at 619 Sixth Avenue, New York City, I shall be able to finish such an one, who has mastered the theory, by a much shorter course of lessons than he would otherwise need, so that it will cost him much less than it would had he never studied the lessons. It has, however, been suggested to me that I have given no instructions on how to meet a very common form of fighting in the United States known as "rough-and-tumble" fighting,[1] and a few observations on that subject may not be amiss in this place.

Rough-and-tumble fighting, as its name implies, contains a good deal of wrestling, and men grapple with each other, roll on the ground, scratch, bite, and gouge, till one or the other gives in. As it commonly takes place among countrymen, schoolboys, and others, the damage inflicted in a rough-and-tumble fight is not serious. The men exchange a few blows, none of any weight, and then grapple and fall. After the grapple it becomes a question of strength and endurance, and the battle ends with a few scratches on either side and much-torn clothes. Between men of the criminal classes, butchers, frontiersmen, and determined, desperate characters of that sort, a rough-and-tumble fight is a very different affair. Such men are full of the most diabolical tricks that can be imagined, and, if they once get a grip on a weaker man, he is nearly sure to lose a finger, an eye, or a nose, and to be bitten or gouged in a horrible manner—in short, to get decidedly the worst of it. Therefore, in dealing with such men—and no gentleman can tell when he may be called on to confront such—there is but one plan to pursue. Hit out the best you know how, keep your antagonist at a distance, and *never allow him to grapple you.* Your right-hand full-arm blow, if you can only get it in, will stop almost any grappler, and your rear leap will keep you out of his way. If you have long hair be especially careful; for the first thing a rough-and-tumble fighter makes for is his enemy's hair, so as to bring the face close to bite at it, or to get one thumb into the comer of the enemy's eye. For this reason gentlemen, liable to get among bad characters when coming home at night, should keep their hair short, unless they feel confident of their ability to take care of it. But, in case of such liability, as may be the case with night editors and reporters, musicians, or actors at theatres and

A boxer parrying the kick of a French **savateur,** *from* **National Police Gazette.**

shows, doctors out after night patients, National Guardsmen coming from a drill, theatre-goers, and club men, I decidedly recommend every gentlemen to carry that useful friend, a stout hickory cane with a hook, of which I shall speak more at length in the next paper.

The subject of the present article is the use of natural weapons alone, and we have learned the principles on which the most important of these—the fist—is employed. The next weapon, and one in which most real rough-and-tumble fighters are proficient, is the foot—the art of kicking. The French have even erected this into a separate style of boxing, which they call the *savate*[2], of which one or two exhibitions have been given in New York. The principles of the *savate* are simple, and it is well that every gentleman should know how to contend against a kicker, as otherwise he may be taken by surprise, and badly injured. Really, kicking is a poor way of fighting against a man who knows how to counteract it; but against a greenhorn it is a terrible method of offense, as a single, well-planted kick in the lower part of the body may kill a man. A kick can be avoided by rear leap, or a step to one side, and the person assaulted can also parry it with the hand or foot, catching at the ankle of the kicker, and throwing him. It requires activity and practice with a friend, both parties, of course, taking off their shoes to prevent injury. In the *savate*, the kick is made with the flat foot, sidewise or to the rear, the kicker wheeling round to kick. A man's leg may be broken by such a blow, if he is not up to the trick. The *savate* boxer generally spars with either foot forward, feints with the fist at the head, then suddenly wheels on the rear heel, and lashes out with the forward foot, half turning his back on his opponent. The kick is to be evaded by activity, or if it cannot, then either parried with the hand, or taken on the side of the thigh, where it hurts least. In teaching the *savate* I use also a parry with the leg for exhibition purposes; but in fighting such a kicker, I should depend principally on the hands, and on closing to in-fighting, where the correct full-arm blows would take effect. There has never been known an instance, where the *savate* has been tried with the gloves against a skillful boxer, in which the *savateur* has not been beaten by the face blows; for the art of kicking is so violent and destructive to the equilibrium that the *savateur* who misses his kick is pretty sure to receive a blow before he can come back to his guard. Therefore, if you happen to come on a bad kicker, keep your wits about you, escape his kicks by activity and rear leap, unless you can surely parry. If you can parry, try to get in one or two good blows before the *savateur* gets away, as he will try to do. This is all I have thought beat to say about the *savate*, which is really only dangerous, where it is a new way of fighting. Once it is known, it amounts to little against a real boxer who strikes a correct blow, still, every gentleman who aims at being accomplished in bodily exercises, should know what to do against a French kicker, or he may find himself killed or maimed by such.

A savateur executes a "coup de pied bas," or kick to the foreleg. From Lemoine's **Traité d'éducation physique,** 1857.

There is another method of kicking, which is practiced in some parts of Wales, which is still more dangerous, though very few men have enough activity to execute it. In this the kicker runs at his enemy, leaps in the air, and dashes both heels in the other's face.[3] There is only one possible defense to this—the rear leap, or side leap. The kicks are too strong to be parried, but, if evaded, they tire out the kicker very soon, and a boxer could then close in and finish him. Therefore, as in the *savate*, my advice is, keep cool, and remember that activity is half the battle.

In some parts of the north of England, kicking in a fight is called "purring,"[4] and the navvies[5] put on special boots, with plates of iron in the toes, called "purring boots," with which they frequently maim

Purring contests, practiced in the close-quarters style in which combatants gripped each other by the belts and shoulders, as depicted in **National Police Gazette.** *Courtesy of William A. Mays, proprietor of* **National Police Gazette.**

each other for life. This is a sickening and brutal way of fighting, which is happily not often met. If ever a gentleman should unhappily be caught by such savages, I know of no weapon against them so good as a pistol.

All kicks can be parried with the leg or knee, and the principles are simple. I shall suppose the pupil standing in boxing position at "guard," the balance on the right hip, the left foot forward, and flexible. Never throw the weight on the forward foot, or a *savateur* will catch you on the shin, and, perhaps, break your leg. The kick, whether from toe or flat foot, will come straight at you, either at your shin or the lower part of your body. You parry it either to the inside or outside, as follows:

I. *Inside Leg Parry.*—As the kick comes, shrink the body back, turning slightly to the right on right heel, and raise the left leg, bent at the

knee, catching the kicker's ankle sidewise with your own leg, anywhere from the knee to the instep, and throwing his kick off to your right or inside. You can now return in two ways: (1.) If he kicked with the left foot, his body is open to a return kick with the parrying leg. (2.) If he kicked with the right, you have him swung round as in counter-cross-parry, and you can either catch his foot with your hands and throw him, or close in, and deliver your best left and right hand blows at his face or body, or both. Closing in is preferable to catching the foot, as a *savateur* will throw himself down on his hands, and kick with the other foot.

II. *Outside Leg Parry.*—Shrink the body back as before, raise the knee and catch the kick sidewise from right to left with your own leg, anywhere from knee to foot, throwing the kick off to your left or outside. You can now return in two ways, as in inside parry: (1.) If he kicked with left leg, you have him swung round as in counter-cross-parry, and can close in with arm blows, or throw him, closing in being preferable. (2.) If he kicked with right leg, his body is open to a return kick with the parrying leg.

These are the two valuable leg parries, of which all others are modifications. You can change and fight with the other foot forward, when the directions are of course reversed. If you find you cannot parry the kick, shrink back the body and take it on the fleshy part of the thigh, where it hurts least. Toe-kicks are the hardest to parry, but the most dangerous to the kicker, as they expose him to a severe sprain, unless he have heavy-soled boots. With light boots, the flat-foot or heel-kick is to be preferred. In kicking contests, the front of the body is the part to be saved, the side and back are the least vulnerable; be prepared, therefore, to wheel rapidly, and always balance on the rear leg, with the forward leg lightly planted, ready to parry, trip, or return kicks. If your enemy is a big, heavy man, use the rear leap and stand on the defensive, so as to tire him out, saving yourself till his kicks are less powerful and rapid. If you get thrown, kick out your best till you get a chance to jump up again. The above directions will show the general principles of the science of kicking.

Next after the foot comes the head, used as a weapon. A single blow with the head will decide almost any fight, if properly put in. The only place I know where men fight scientifically with the head is in Denmark. Negroes do not fight; they merely butt heads to try which is hardest. The Danes call a blow with the head a "skalle," and the Germans call it a "Danish kiss." The Danes sometimes have fights where it is agreed to use the head only. The principles are simple. The men circle round each other much as in Græco-Roman wrestling. The aim is to get the hands under the opponent's arms and on his shoulders, then to dash the head in his face. The side of the head is used, near the top, where the skull is thickest. One blow, well sent in, will break any man's nose and teeth, and knock him senseless. The parry is, however, simple and efficacious. Spread the hands before the face, prevent your enemy's grip, and push away his head if he gets it. It then becomes a question of main strength of arm. Break away at any cost, by striking up with the knee at an enemy who gets this grip on you, and never fight with a Dane if you can help it. I never found but two natural fighters in my life that I could not sicken, and they were two Danes of Copenhagen, who seemed to be proof against any amount of punishment, including a five-pound stone in the face, sent with all my force. They wanted to rob me, and I fought my very best, but nothing seemed to hurt them, and I had to run at last. Therefore, I advise all people to keep clear of fighting with Danes and Norwegians, for the last are as bad as the first.

Francis Langdon head-butts a New York City police officer in the African American style. The incident occurred in 1879, on the corner of Sullivan and Broome streets, roughly ten blocks from where Monstery's Bleecker Street academy had been located. Courtesy of William A. Mays, proprietor of **National Police Gazette.**

If a man fights you in the negro style[6], trying to butt you in the stomach, he is not so much to be feared. There is no science in him.[7] Wait for him, right foot foremost, and strike up the right knee with all your force in his face, holding both your hands open to shield the "mark," and stooping forward. The knee will sicken any man, even a negro, from butting, unless he be enormously powerful and you very weak, in which case it is life or death, and a pistol the best protection.

These are all the hints that I have thought best to give concerning rough-and-tumble fighting, to show how its dangers are to be avoided in case a gentleman gets caught in such a scrape, where everything is

A butting contest depicted in **Harper's Weekly,** *1874.*

fair. Generally, my advice is keep clear of rough-and-tumble fighters, or shoot them down, for they are horrible beings, bent on murdering or maiming their fellow creatures, and worthy of no better treatment than men give to wolves—that is bullet or steel.

Above all things, never lose your presence of mind, and never consider yourself unarmed even if confronted by an armed man, for almost anything can be made into a weapon if properly used. An umbrella is a fearful weapon if used with both hands like a bayonet. It will parry the blows of a big bully, and you can return him a stab in the face or breast or stomach that will settle him. A lady can defend herself from outrage with her parasol in the same way. If she struck a ruffian over the head with it, he would laugh at her, but I remember a certain girl who killed a ruffian who assaulted her by a stab with the point of her parasol. The lightest cane is dangerous, used in this way. If you have none of these, and a robber demands your money, tell him you will give it to him. Take it out and then throw it edgewise in his face. A trade dollar will make a dent half an inch deep in an oak board, properly thrown, and a quarter of a dollar will stun a man.[8] In fact you are never unarmed if you have money in your pocket. I have saved both life and money from a cocked pistol, before this, by knowing how to throw my loose change, and by preserving my presence of mind.

Endnotes

1 Rough-and-tumble fighting had its genesis in the American colonies during the eighteenth century and reached its pinnacle in New York City during the mid-1800s. An 1870 article summarized the style as follows: "There are two classes of professional fighters. The members of one submit to the recognized rules of 'a fair, stand-up' encounter. There is a ring in which the combatants meet. They are allowed to use no weapons but their fists, foul blows are prohibited, and the affair is conducted according to regulations . . . The other professional fighters are of a lower order. They fall upon each other in 'rough-and-tumble' fashion, and bite, and tear, and gouge, after the manner of the dogs their companionship disgraces." *Brooklyn Daily Eagle*, Aug. 6, 1870, 2.

During the 1870s, when Monstery taught in Manhattan, numerous accounts of local rough-and-tumble fights appeared in the pages of the *New York Times* and *Brooklyn Daily Eagle*. The famous rough-and-tumble fight between Bill "The Butcher" Poole and John Morrissey had taken place on Christopher Street in 1854, not far from Monstery's Bleecker Street school. Monstery probably felt that there was a very real danger of his students encountering such fighters. To this end he employed John Charles Collins, a veteran of numerous rough-and-tumble encounters, to teach pugilism at his Sixth Avenue academy. During his service in the U.S. Navy at age twenty-two, Monstery himself was forced to battle a rough-and-tumble fighter named Bliss; he conceded the match when the latter attempted to gouge him. See Capt. Frederick Whittaker, *The Sword Prince* (New York: M. J. Ivers & Co.), 10–11, and *The Daily Inter Ocean*, Dec. 25, 1878.

2 *Savate*, also known as *Boxe Française*, is a form of French street fighting that developed during the nineteenth century in Paris and Marseilles, and is still practiced to this day.

3 A possible reference to this style, dubbed "the running punce," appeared in the *Hampshire Telegraph and Sussex Chronicle*, Sept. 9, 1874: "The effect of this kick is graphically described by a witness. 'Every limb of Metcalf's body shot out, as if he had given up.' And so he had, for he died the next morning at 10 o'clock, the 'running punce' having fractured his skull."

4 "Purring" was practiced in several regions of the British Isles, including Lancashire, Derbyshire (as well as other parts of the English midlands), Wales, Devon, and Cornwall. It was eventually brought to the United States, where it was practiced among the coal miners of Pennsylvania. During the late nineteenth century, high-profile purring contests took place in Scranton, Pittsburgh, Reading, and Phoenixville. In January 1883, a particularly brutal and bloody match was fought in Camden, New Jersey, between Robert Tavish and David McWilliams of Luzerne County. In its Jan. 13, 1883 account of the fight, the *New York Times* reported, "It is really scientific shin-kicking, and the victory belongs to the contestant who is most agile and the best able to stand punishment. The sport originated among the Cornish miners." Hopping around "like a dancing master," Tavish triumphed in the twenty-third round after kicking McWilliams's legs until they "were as raw as beefsteak." *National Police Gazette*, Feb. 3, 1883, 13.

In England, purring involved kicking "on every part of the body, in all possible situations, and of squeezing the throat, or 'throtling' to the very verge of death." In Lancashire, the style was sometimes referred to as "up and down fighting." See Edward Baines, *The History, Directory, and Gazetteer, of the County Palatine of Lancaster* (Liverpoole: W. Wales & Co., 1821), 537.

5 A Victorian slang term applied to various types of manual laborers; during Monstery's era, it was especially applied to railway workers.

6 Accounts of African American head-butting matches can be found as far back as the eighteenth century. The origin of this tradition lies in West Africa, where tribes such as the Mpongwe were known to fight by "butting each other in the stomach with their heads." In the American south, practitioners adopted the rituals of the duel, as described by former slave Henry Bibb: "Before fighting, the parties choose their seconds to stand by them while fighting; a ring or a circle is formed to fight in, and no one is allowed to enter the ring while they are fighting, but their seconds...The blows are made by kicking, knocking, and butting their heads; they grab each other by the ears, and jam their heads together like sheep." During the late nineteenth century, public butting contests were reported in San Francisco and Greenville, North Carolina. See *National Police Gazette*, Feb. 4, 1893 and Aug. 9, 1879; Robert H. Milligan, *The Fetish Folk of West Africa* (London: Fleming H. Revell Co., 1912), 36; and Henry Bibb, *Narrative of the Life and Adventures of Henry Bibb, an American Slave* (New York: printed by author, 1850).

7 While Monstery's comment might sound derisive, numerous period accounts show that African American butting contests were not typically decided by skill, but rather, physical endurance and ability to withstand pain—often to the point of death. This did not mean, however, that no technique was involved. During the American Revolution, when a secret patriot expeditionary force cornered British Major General Richard Prescott at his Rhode Island headquarters, a black boatman named Jack Sisson broke down the general's door with his head. Sixty years later,

one of the black servants of the Lafayette Guards, a New York regiment touring Boston, impressed onlookers "with his remarkable butting." See Jeffrey Bolster, *Black Jacks: African American Seamen in the Age of Sail* (Cambridge, MA: Harvard University Press, 1997), 119–120.

8 Monstery used this trick against an armed robber who confronted him in Mexico. As his biography recounted, "It was an old trick of his to bury a gold *onza* in a plank so deep that it could not be pulled out with the fingers, and his blow inflicted such pain on the villain that he dropped his pistol and screamed out." Whittaker, *The Sword Prince,*, 31.

This week closes Col. Monstery's Instructions to Gentlemen desirous of becoming familiar with methods of self-defense. Next week he will explain the use of the cane, following with the art of fencing . . .

—*The Spirit of the Times,* February 23, 1878

XII.

THE USE *of the* CANE.

The first step made by natural and savage man toward civilization is the adoption of an artificial weapon, to compensate for the inferiority of those with which he is furnished by nature. Lacking the powerful jaws of the wolf, and the terrible claws of the tiger, the horns of the cattle, and the hoofs of the horse, he possesses in his hands and brains the faculty of invention, and the first use to which he puts it is the construction of a weapon. This comes before clothing and shelter, for food is the first necessity of the animal man, and without a weapon he cannot obtain animal food, but must live on roots and insects. The first mark of intelligence found in the most degraded savages is a weapon, and the first weapon he makes is a stick or club, a straight branch torn from a tree. As he progresses, the weapon becomes either a lance or a battle-axe. A thick, heavy club is cleft at the end, and a sharp wedge of stone stuck in the cleft, when the savage possesses a war-club or *celt*, the universal weapon of savage nations. We find celts of rough-chipped stone, of polished stone, and of bronze, one following after the other, in the remains of extinct peoples in Denmark, France, and Ireland, and under the lake dwellings of Switzerland. We find the Indians of our own prairies using the same war-club, when our earlier travelers crossed the continent of North America; and the savages of Polynesia carry the war-club today as their fathers handed it down to them, with a heavy knob at the end, while no nation has been found so savage as not to possess a long stick, with a point sharpened in the fire, and fashioned into a spear or lance, even where bows and arrows are unknown. As civilization advances, and the sword and bow replace the club, the spear retains its place but the club becomes a peaceful staff, and finally, in the highest civilization, we see the staff universally used as a walking-cane, light or heavy, as the owner pleases.

In this chapter I propose to treat of the use of the cane, the proper companion of every gentleman. Boxing will get a gentleman out of a great many scrapes into which he may fall, but in some parts of the Union he will come across men who habitually carry knives or pistols and in such a case a stout walking-stick, if he knows how to use it, may save his own life, and—what I consider more important—prevent the necessity of his taking the life of another. It may seem strange to some that I, who have passed my time in the profession of arms, and have lived so much in Spanish-America, where the use of weapons is universal and duels of everyday occurrence, should have a horror of taking life; and yet I can honestly say that I have always avoided it, except where there was an absolute certainty that the question lay between my own life and that of another who sought to kill me. For this reason I have always avoided the use of the pistol, except in battle. You cannot spare a man's life with the pistol, and no generosity can be shown therewith. You must kill him or he kills you. With the cane it is different. Many are the pistols and knives that I have struck from the hands of men by a smart blow on the wrist with a cane, and many are the murderous brawls I have prevented in this way. As a queller of disturbances, I know of nothing better than a hickory or ash stick. Like the fist, it is a weapon with which an opponent may be conquered without injury to his life. I do not recommend a heavy club or cudgel, except in the country, at night, where one is liable to be attacked by savage dogs, and where a single heavy blow is all that is required.

In such a case a heavy stick is useful, but where anything else is the object, a light, tough hickory stick, with a hook to it, is the best of all. The hook is an important part of the cane. It doubles its usefulness, serves as a handle to rest on when it is used as a staff, prevents its slipping out of the hand when it is used as a weapon, and serves as a sling when you do not wish to handle the cane. With a hook to his cane, no man need ever abandon it, for he can always hang it over his left arm when not in use, so as to be ready to catch it instantly with the right.

Above all things, I wish my pupils to remember that loaded canes and sword canes are only fit for assassins, and not for brave men. For a sudden assault by stealth on an unarmed man, they are the weapon, but for nothing else, as they possess no powers of defense. An active man, with a stout, light hickory stick, can beat any man with a sword-cane, for he can parry the thrust, and break the slender weapon, or the holder's wrist, with a sharp blow. A thin, elastic cane, with a leaden knob, is a still poorer weapon of defense, as it can parry no heavy blows, while its own blows are easily parried with a hickory stick. Heavy lignum vitæ or ironwood canes are also bad, because they are unmanageable. They strike a heavy blow, but it can be parried with a hickory stick, and the lighter weapon can get in three blows to one of the other. Especially is it difficult with a heavy weapon to guard the wrist and hand, so that a man trusting to such a weapon may find himself disabled by a quick antagonist, who parries all his heavy blows, and returns with cuts at the wrist and temple.

Against a knife or knives, there is no weapon so good as a stout stick, and as one true incident is worth a column of maxims, I will here give something that happened to myself many years ago, which will give an idea of what may be done by a strong, active man, with a hickory cane. The whole story will be found in the Philadelphia papers, about the date of which I write, and can be verified thereby, as I write from memory only. It was on the evening of May 3, 1851, that I was induced to take a trip from Philadelphia to one of the suburbs called Frankfort, in company with a Spaniard who rejoiced in the name of Jose Jesus de Gomez. This man, as I afterwards found out, had a secret animosity against me, though the exact reason was never quite clear. It was, probably, partly political, as I afterwards heard that he was in the secret service of the Spanish Government, while I was at that time quite intimate with poor Lopez, who was executed in Cuba for attempted insurrection. I have also reason to believe that jealousy figured as another cause of his hatred, as we were rivals for the affections of the same lady.[1] At all events, this man pretended the most extravagant friendship for me, and, although something in his manner caused me, at times, to suspect he was playing a part, he at last lulled my suspicions and I thought him my friend. On the evening in question we went out to Frankfort, and stayed there till it was dark. I had intended to return by the same stage as that in which we went out, but Gomez so managed that we overstayed the time, and the last stage had gone before we were ready. I then proposed hiring a carriage, but to this Gomez objected, insisting that it was a lovely night, that it was no use throwing away money, and that we could walk home together. I will own that I had begun to entertain some vague suspicion of the man on the way, owing to one thing: I noticed that he carried with him a long knife in a sheath under the left breast of his coat. It was one of the most beautiful knives I ever saw, with an ivory handle and a very long blade of remarkably fine steel, with which one could split a silver dollar at a blow. I had noticed this knife, and yet, somehow, I associated no thought of danger with it. In those days the carrying of weapons was very common, and, as I had often seen this knife before, I thought no more of it as we walked home.

We left Frankfort behind and strolled along toward Philadelphia. I remember that at first the same vague suspicion, which I have before mentioned, possessed me for a time, so that I insisted on walking arm-in-arm with Gomez, taking his right arm with my left. I, myself, had no weapon except my light, hickory walking-cane with a hook to it. I had forgotten to say that one circumstance which excited my suspicion in the early part of our walk was this: I had, in those times, great skill in stone throwing, and frequently threw up a stone in the air, striking it with another before it reached the ground. I had been showing this trick and he tried it, too, but, instead of throwing away from me, threw a large stone toward me, very narrowly missing my head. It seemed singular to me, but, nevertheless, I laid it all to his clumsiness, and forgot it again. At last, as I had hold of his arm, he swore so much friendship for me that I grew ashamed of my suspicions, and thought to myself I was a fool. I let go his arm and we walked on side by side, my left to his right, through the silent starlight night.

Suddenly, without a word of warning, he whipped out his knife and made a furious stab for my heart over my left arm. I knew it by the flash of the blade in the starlight, and, with the common instinct of humanity, I shrunk back and half raised my bent arm as a shield. Flash and motion were instantaneous, and then the knife went through my arm, half way between shoulder and elbow, striking the bone, as I realized in a moment from the numbing shock and the sense of sickness I experienced. The point even entered my breast, but did not pierce far.

Of course I found all these details afterwards, but for the moment I only felt the blow, and I reeled back, everything dancing before my eyes. Instinctively I kept flourishing my stick, shouting and retreating, defending myself by making rapid *moulinets*[2] and falling back from before Gomez, who seemed now to be perfectly frantic as he rushed at me. Then he stopped and whistled, when out jumped two more men, Spaniards both, with knives, and there I was on that lonely road with a hickory stick fighting three men armed with knives, and determined to kill me to hide their own crime. I realized all this in a flash. I knew Gomez; he knew I knew him, and that if he failed to kill me Philadelphia would be too hot for him; so no wonder he was desperate. But, before his friends came up, I had a moment's breathing spell, and the stunned sick feeling had worn off, so that I had regained my presence of mind and remembered that I had a stick. In my turn I attacked, first one, then the other, jumping back and always aiming to have only one at a time in front of me, by getting the others behind him. Then I kept my stick going with quick cuts at the wrist and temple of each man—crack! crack! as hard as I could, and hitting every time, as they could not parry with their short knives. I sent the knife flying out of Gomez's hand, and must have nearly broken his wrist, for I remember today how he shrieked out: "*Cristo! Carajo!*" as he held his wrist with the other hand and backed out. Then right into the midst of our fight drove up a farmer's wagon, and I was separated from my enemies.

I shouted out to the driver to help me, as they were trying to murder me, but he, probably thinking it to be a scheme of some gang of footpads, whipped up and drove on faster than ever. Then, when I looked, my enemies had disappeared. They had evidently been frightened by the coming of the wagon, and thought they were discovered, so they made off. Then I found I had got three stabs altogether, the last two in the forearm, and, I think, all given by the same man in my first confusion and surprise, before I recovered my presence of mind and used my stick.

I will not trouble the reader here with the details of how I got home, after a walk to the toll-gate, where a wagon was procured. My

Spanish knife fencers, in **Manual de Esgrima y Duelo,** *1892.*

principal assailant was arrested, and I recovered in two months' time, but I carry the scars today, the largest of all being of that first stab where Gomez splintered the bone of my arm.

My object in telling the story is not that of braggadocio, but to show what a weapon exists in a hickory cane. Had I been in full strength, my victory over three men would not have been so very unusual or surprising, with my long weapon against their short ones, my training as an athlete against their inexperience, my strength being greater than any of theirs. But as it was, that first stab of Gomez reduced me to their level and below it in strength, and left me only my weapon and my skill. The result was that the hickory cane proved itself the master of the knife and saved my life. Having shown that much, it is time I told you how it is to be used, and this I shall try to do next week.

Endnotes

1 Monstery's future wife, the Cuban-born Carmen Xiques (1831–1908).
2 Circular cuts with the broadsword or saber.

In his continuation of his instructions on the use of the cane, this week, Col. Monstery goes into detail, and as far as can be done in type, makes his readers masters of this handy and useful weapon. It is evident that when a man can place himself behind a curtain of revolving and gyrating canes, like the hero of the last illustration, he becomes impregnable.

—*The Spirit of the Times*, March 16, 1878

XIII.

THE USE *of the* CANE

(continued).

The use of the cane depends on principles resembling those of the broadsword or sabre, with one important difference. The sword has, or should have, a guard to cover the hand from injury, therefore, the parries with a sword can be made with the point up, the hand remaining in the same position at all times, so as to secure the grand secret of defense—*economy of motions.* The cane, on the other hand, having no guard, it is necessary that all blows should be taken on it in such a manner that they may be diverted away from the hand, and therefore all guards[1] in cane exercise are made with the point down. The first necessity in the handling of the cane is to secure a supple and easy play of the wrist, so that the blows may be delivered without the necessity of drawing back the arm.

The lessons with the cane are started, just as those in boxing and fencing are commenced, from the position of a soldier, which we will recapitulate, with the difference that the pupil holds his cane in his right hand. The instructor commands:

Attention!

The pupil stands with his heels on a line and together; toes turned out at an angle of sixty degrees or thereabouts; knees straight, without stiffness; body erect on the hips, inclining a little forward; arms hanging naturally, elbows near the body; palm of the left hand to the side, little finger on the seam of the pantaloons; right hand grasping the cane near the hook, the point of the cane sloping to the front, toward the ground, the thumb and forefinger locked round the cane, the other fingers loosely closed on the heel of the hand, wrist supple; shoulders square to the front; head erect, chin drawn in without stiffness, eyes fixed on the centre of the adversary, at the height of the breast.

The instructor next commands:

1. Ready. 2. Two.

This is executed by the numbers as follows:

1) At the word "Ready," face to the left, by turning on the left heel at right angles to the adversary or instructor, position otherwise unchanged, the head turning to the right as the body moves to the left, so as not to lose sight of the instructor.

2) At the word "Two," the right foot is moved straight toward the instructor, and planted lightly, the toe pointing toward him, the left foot at right angles to the right, the distance between the feet about twelve inches, according to height; the left arm is bent, the palm of the left hand resting on the left hip, thumb to the front; the body balances on the left hip, the knees slightly bent; the right hand is carried over to the inside of the right thigh, and turned, the back of the hand to the body, the point of the cane resting on the ground, the inside of the right foot as in the figure. The right shoulder points toward the adversary, and the body is

1. Ready. 2. Two.

"effaced" as much as possible, the side being presented instead of the breast, the left arm sheltered behind the body, having only the right side exposed to blows.

[*Remarks.*—The pupil is now in position to come to guard or to strike any of the blows that follow. He has assumed an attitude that would not attract attention in a crowd, but he is ready for anything that comes. This is the position that I have assumed more than once when some man was talking to me menacingly, with his hand on his pistol pocket. Suspecting nothing, he has at last drawn his weapon, but before he could cover me therewith, he has received a severe blow on the wrist, which sent the pistol flying. To strike this blow from this position, step out with the right foot, and bring round the hand, the point of the cane describing a semicircle from the ground, diagonally upward to the opponent's hip, aiming for his wrist. It makes a strong backhanded blow, to be followed by others aimed at his temples. Remember that, in cane exercise, all blows should be aimed at the right wrist, or at the side of the head and face of the antagonist, with a view to disable or stun him. Body blows are useless; they do not hurt enough to disable, and the whole object of cane exercise is to disable an opponent, so that he cannot hurt you. Blows at the legs are worse than useless against a skillful adversary, as they are not only easily parried, but they expose the user to a severe blow on the head or wrist, if the opponent chooses either to take the leg blow, or to withdraw the threatened leg, instead of parrying[2] the blow.]

MOULINETS.

From the position of "Ready," the pupil is taught the moulinet[3] and espadoning[4,] as follows:

The instructor commands:

1. First Moulinet. 2. Two. 3. Three. 4. Four.

1) At the word "moulinet," extend the hand toward the instructor, with the nails up at the height of the eyes, back of the hand down, point of the cane to the instructor, and a little higher than the hand, which holds the cane in the thumb and forefinger lock, the other fingers being loosely closed.

2) At the word "two," lower the point of the cane, by bending the wrist without bending the arm, loosening all the fingers but the first and thumb, and rapidly describe a complete circle (*moulinet* means "mill-wheel") around the hand, to the right of and near the body, the cane passing close to the right elbow and back, thence returning down to the front.

3) At the word "three," turn the back of the hand up and to the left, nails down, and again lower the point of the cane, describing a second circle, to the left of and near the body, the cane passing the breast and returning down to the front.

4) Return to ready.

Moulinets.

The second moulinet is a reversal of the first, and is executed by the commands:

1. Second moulinet. 2. Two. 3. Three. 4. Four.

   1) At the word "moulinet" extend the hand as in the first moulinet, nails up.

   2) At the word "two," raise the point of the cane and describe a reverse circle, behind the back and elbows, ending by the point coming upward to the front.

   3) At the word "three," turn the hand as in No. 3 of the first moulinet, and raise the point of the cane, describing the reverse circle in front of the breast, ending by the point coming upward to the front.

   4) At the word "four," return to ready.

[*Remarks.*—The use of the moulinets is to supple the wrist and accustom the pupil to strike without exposing the arm. If a man cannot execute the moulinets correctly and rapidly, he can never handle a cane properly. The moulinets must be persevered in and practiced constantly as a foundation to everything else. The instructor will command, "two," "three," "two," "three," on occasion, without ending the moulinet by "four" till the close of the exercise, and should see that the pupil executes the moulinet with enough force to make the stick whistle loudly, without any bending of the arm.]

The next exercise is denominated "espadoning," and is an improvement on the moulinets, as it simulates the blows more closely. The instructor commands:

1. First espadon. 2. Two. 3. Three. 4. Four.

1) At the command "espadon," extend the hand, nails up, as high as the head, arm quite straight, wrist bent, so that the point of the cane is lower than the hand.

2) At the word "two," describe the first half of the first moulinet, retaining the cane between the locked thumb and forefinger, as in the figure, the other fingers loose, as the point descends. As it rises to the perpendicular, close all the fingers firmly on the cane, and end the espadon with a whistling blow, the point lower than the hand.

3) At the word "three," turn the hand, nails down, back of the hand to the left and up. Execute second half of first moulinet 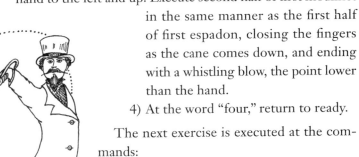 in the same manner as the first half of first espadon, closing the fingers as the cane comes down, and ending with a whistling blow, the point lower than the hand.

4) At the word "four," return to ready.

The next exercise is executed at the commands:

1. Second espadon. 2. Two. 3. Three. 4. Four.

1) Extend the cane as in second moulinet, point lower than the hand, which is at height of head.

2) Execute the espadon in reverse, ending with upward blow, that whistles, point lower than hand.

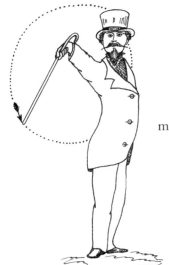

1. First espadon. 2. Two.

3) Turn the hand and execute second half of espadon in reverse, as before.

4) Return to ready.

[*Remarks.*—Espadoning is borrowed from the sword exercise, and is meant to simulate the blows exactly. It accustoms the pupil to keep his hand high in striking, and to end his blow with the point lower than the hand in all high cuts. This is important, for two reasons: 1st. It makes a perfect blow, and compels the enemy to come to a perfect parry. 2nd. It leaves the hand in a position to guard against the return blow. If the hand is low, the return blow is sure to catch you, as the upper body and head are open. This makes the danger of striking at an enemy's legs, as the hand must be low to strike at them.]

After the espadoning is perfectly executed, the instructor teaches the blows, which are four in number, as seen in the diagram below, the fifth being merely a formula, straight down at the top of the head, never used by a skillful cane player, as it is easily guarded, and if it reaches the enemy only smashes his hat.

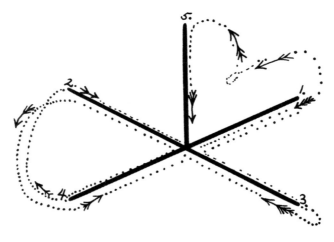

THE BLOWS.

The pupil being in position of ready, the instructor commands:

1. Strike one. 2. Two. 3. Three. 4. Four. 5. Five. 6. Ready.

1) Step forward with the right foot, lifting the toe and plant-ing the foot as far forward as possible, without losing the balance. At the same time, stretch out the right hand, back of the hand to the left, arm quite straight, hand the height of the head, the cane firmly grasped in the lock of thumb and forefinger, point back by the left shoulder. Sweep the point around, upward, turning the hand, nails up; then strike diagonally downward, as in diagram, which shows by the arrows and dotted lines the path of the cane.

2) As the cane comes to the end of the blow, sweep it around in a semi-circle, as in diagram, and strike down on the opposite side, back of hand up.

3) At close of blow, turn the hand, nails up, and strike diagonally upward.

4) At close of blow, sweep the point round, as in diagram, and strike again, diagonally upward, on the opposite side.

5) At close of blow, throw the point over, back to the right shoulder, and then strike straight down, ending with the cane at the height of the head, the point lower than the hand.

6) At the word "ready," spring back to that position.

[*Remarks.*—The blows are really only four in number, but I have allowed the fifth to go into the diagram for the sake of making the guards to all the blows as simple as possible to persons who know nothing at all of cane play. A little thought will show that there is no fifth blow. A blow at the top of the head must be given with the nails either up to the left or down to the right. In one position it is a first blow, in the other a second blow. All blows coming from the right downward, at whatever angle, are comprehended in first blow; all from the left down in second blow, all from right upward in third blow; and all from left upward In fourth blow. For this reason it is obvious that they form a circle of four quadrants, in the centre of which stands the adversary. He, on his part, sees you in a similar circle, and can strike his blows at you from any point in that circle. This thought will help you to understand the next picture, which represents the guards.]

The Guards.

After the blows have been thoroughly taught to the pupil, so that he executes them as rapidly as the espadons, making every blow whistle sharply with the wrist alone, the arm straight, and the hand as high as the top of the head, the pupil is put in the position of ready. The guards are then taught by the commands.

1. Guard—2. First Guard—3. Second Guard—4. Third Guard—5. Fourth Guard—6. Fifth Guard—7. Guard!

1) At the word "guard," extend the hand as in picture, back of the hand up and to the left, arm at height of shoulder, hand to the right, cane pointing diagonally downward, the point on the perpendicular line dividing the antagonist's body into two halves. This is a perfect guard against fourth blow at the wrist or arm, the most exposed spot in a cane player, and, therefore, the first to be protected.

2) At the word "first guard," carry the hand up to the left as in picture, which shows position of cane against all kinds of first blows. The blows are indicated by the arrows connected by the brackets.

3) At word "second guard," carry the hand to the right, the cane as in picture, against all second blows.

4) At command "third guard," carry the hand to the left at height of shoulder, holding cane as in picture against all kinds of third blows.

The guards.

5) At command "fourth guard," return to guard against all kinds of fourth blows.

6) At command "fifth guard," carry hand above head as in picture so that the blows will slide on to the left.

7) Return to guard.

[*Remarks.*—After the guards are explained, the instructor should make the pupil execute the blows and take them on his own guards. Then the operation should be reversed, the instructor striking, the pupil guarding. It will be noticed in the picture that the canes cross the blows at right angles, and surround the man with a wall of defense. Against blows at the leg, if you choose to parry them, third and fourth guards are lowered as in the figure, but generally it is better to withdraw the leg and strike at the antagonist's face or wrist.]

The pupil has now learned the blows and guards, and will next be practiced in the feints[5] and returns.[6] The simple feints are practiced as follows:

1. Feint One at head, strike Two at wrist.
2. Feint One, strike Four at wrist.
3. Feint One, strike Three at face.
4. Feint Two, strike One at face.
5. Feint Two, strike Three at face.

The double feints are generally executed with three blows, two of which are to draw the guards to a certain position, while the third comes straight up the line of the cane past the point, so as to prevent a guard being formed in time. The following will give an idea of the principle:

1. Feint One, Four, strike Three at face under the guard.
2. Feint Two, One, strike Three at face under the guard.

Other feints may be invented on same principle, the first and second high, third low, or vice versa.

Next come the returns, which are as follows:

1. Guard first blow, return first;
2. Guard first, return second;
3. Guard first, return third;
4. Guard first, return fourth;
5. Guard second, and return, successively, first, second, third, and fourth;
6. Guard third, return, successively, all the blows;
7. Guard fourth, return, successively, all the blows.

These returns should be practiced frequently, to secure quickness. They explain themselves. After they have been fully practiced, free play may be taken, in which each party tries to out-time the other by feints, and uses all he knows.

My general advice for cane-play is simple. Practice with a friend with light canes, and use a glove with padded knuckles to save the hand from injury. If you can procure broadsword masks, also arm guards and fencing gloves, you can use full-sized hickory canes and hit as hard as you like; if not, put on hats, and agree to strike at the hat instead of the face, striking lightly with light canes. Remember, however, that a cane is not a sword, nor to be used like one. I have given you my style, which is founded on reason and common sense, but, when you go to exhibitions, you will see other styles, and you may think that what is taught here is incomplete for want of what you see there. You will see men feint at the head and end with a rap at the thigh, while the audience applauds it and calls the play "single-stick." In fact, it is no true stick-play at all, but a cross between the broad-sword and stick. In cane-play there are really only two places to strike at—head and forearm or knuckles. If you choose to hit at your enemy's thigh or body, he will take it and give you a bad one on wrist or face, if he is at all smart. For the same reason, as I do not mention leg blows, I leave out thrusts with the cane. They are easily parried, and expose the thruster to a severe blow on the wrist, if his enemy parries on the wrist. Moreover, there are only two places where they will hurt enough to disable a man, the eyes or the "mark," neither of them easy to reach. With the two-handed or quarter-staff the case is different, as we shall see in our next chapter.

Endnotes

1 A guard is defined as "that position of person and weapon which is the most ready for both attack and defence." Alfred Hutton, *Fixed Bayonets* (London: Clowes & Sons, 1890), 145.

2 A parry is defined as "the movement of the weapon which wards off or stops a thrust or a cut." Hutton, *Fixed Bayonets*, 148.

3 A circular cut with the broadsword or saber. Depending upon the type of weapon and style of fencing, moulinets could be executed from the wrist, elbow, or shoulder. Here, Monstery instructs the reader to moulinet with the cane from the wrist.

4 The word "espadon" is taken from the obsolete French, and refers to a broadsword or saber. Hutton, *Fixed Bayonets*, 143.

5 Feints are "simulated attacks made at various points in order to draw the parry, while the real attack is directed at the opening left by it." Hutton, *Fixed Bayonets*, 143.

6 A return is "a hit delivered immediately after having parried an attack." Hutton, *Fixed Bayonets*, 150.

Col. Monstery gives instruction in the use of the *Alpenstock* as a weapon this week. We trust it will not induce our readers to rush to the mountainous regions of Europe, and make combative "holy shows" of themselves, like the figure in the last illustration, hitting the head of a peaceful Swiss, wherever they can see one.

—*The Spirit of the Times*, March 23, 1878

XIV.
THE USE *of the* STAFF.

The cane, to be used with one hand, is the common assistant, defense, and weapon, of civilized man, in the town and in flat countries. When he goes to the mountains, he finds that the cane is too short and light to be used as a help in climbing, wherefore, mountaineers almost invariably adopt some form of long two-handed staff to assist their steps. Climbing is, of course, infinitely harder than walking. Any man not an invalid or cripple can walk four miles in an hour on a level plain, but no man has yet been found who could climb a mountain four miles high in an hour, or five or six hours either. A long staff, as high as a man's head, forms a great help to a climber. He puts it down before him and then leans on it with both hands, so that he distributes his weight between his arms and legs, four points instead of two. When he stops for breath, he can lean on a long staff when he could not on a short one. If the staff has a hook at one end, he can catch it over rocks and roots above his head and pull himself up by its aid. Such a staff, with an iron spike at the other end, is used by the mountaineers of Switzerland and the Tyrol, and every tourist who goes there to climb the mountains gets one. It is called an *Alpenstock*, which in English is simply an alp-stick or cliff-stick, that is, a climbing-stick or staff. In countries near high mountains, among the foot-hills, the crook and spike are seldom used, but the long staff is almost always retained. In some flat countries, where ditches are common and wide, another kind of long staff is used—the leaping pole. This is quite common in some parts of France, the marshy portion of La Vendée especially, and in Lincolnshire, England, the "fen country," as it is called. In another district of the south of France—the Landes—the peasants walk on stilts, and use staffs about twelve feet long.

In the middle ages, just before, during, and immediately after the crusades, it was very common for men to vow pilgrimages to the Holy Land or to the shrine of some saint. These pilgrims always went on foot and begged their way by the conditions of their vow. They carried no weapons, and their only assistant was a staff. Most of them had to cross mountains as well as plains in the course of their journeys, so they needed a staff which would serve them for either purpose. All these reasons combined to make the long staff more common than the short stick in Europe during the middle ages, and in England, particularly, it became the universal companion of every peasant and yeoman, its use lasting until within two hundred years ago, or till the disuse of armor.

Naturally, besides its use as a staff and leaping-pole, its capacity as a weapon made it quite a favorite with the sturdy countrymen of England who were prohibited by severe laws from wearing swords, the exclusive privilege of "gentlemen" in the old sense of the word, that is, of noble ancestry or free from any trade or handicraft for at least three generations. As long as Sir John and Lord Clarence kept to their shining weapons, Hodge kept to his staff, and the real fact was, that the staff could beat the sword any day in good hands. A man can, of course, strike a harder blow with both hands than with one, and the long staff required two hands to wield it. Therefore, in the early times, when the barons found that Hodge, with his big stick, could beat down their single-handed swords, they invented the great two-handed sword, the most terrible weapon ever used in single combat, and used it just as the staff was used, thereby beating the yeoman at his own game.

It has struck me that a few words on the use of this two-handed staff may not be uninteresting at the present day. Its use has nearly vanished from England, but it is still quite common in the South of France, in the Pyreneean provinces, and in all the mountainous parts of Europe; and as Americans are always traveling in these countries nowadays, and always liable to get into trouble with the people, it may be useful to know how to handle a long staff as well as a short one. I have placed the figures in the cuts in mediaeval costume, copied from thirteenth century manuscripts, because the scientific use of the staff dates from those times. Staff exercises are still taught in Denmark and Holstein, or were when I was a youth, to the peasant *landwehr* for use in case of riot against mobs, in case the men should be summoned so hastily that arms could not be issued to them. A line of resolute lusty fellows, in open order, with big staves, could clear the way through any crowd not provided with firearms.

The two-handed staff was called in England the "quarter-staff," from the manner in which it was at first always held in the guard, one hand in the middle of the staff, the other half-way to the end, so that a quarter of the staff was always below the hand. The modern staff-exercise is a little different, but begins in the same way, and I shall, therefore, lose no more time in talking about it, but commence with the exercise.

THE QUARTER-STAFF EXERCISE.

The instructor places the pupils in open order, facing to the front, and about four feet apart, standing in the position of a soldier, by the commands: *1. Fall in for Staff exercise! 2. Take intervals! 3. Front!* At the first command the pupils range themselves in file, one behind the other, according to height. At the second they step off till the requisite interval is gained. At the third they face the instructor.

He then explains the meaning of the following changes, and commands successively:

On Guard!

Wheel on the left heel to the right, and throw back the right foot about eighteen inches, according to height, to secure a steady position, feet at right-angles to each other.

Extend!

Double the distance between the feet by advancing the forward foot.

Guard!

Return to first position.

Advance!

Double the distance between the feet as in "Extend," and then bring up the rear foot to "Guard" distance.

Retreat!

Double the distance between the feet by stepping back with rear the foot, then drawing back the forward foot to "Guard" distance.

The instructor then commands the "double advance" and retreat, and the same "at will" as in boxing, and finally gives the word:

Front—Change!

At the word "Change" wheel on the left heel to the left front, throwing the right foot forward, the interval between the feet remaining the same.

Front—Change!

Wheel on right heel to the right front, throwing the left foot forward same distance.

Rear—Change!

At the word "Change" wheel on right heel to the left, throwing the left foot back, same distance.

Rear—Change!

Wheel on left heel to the right, throwing the right foot back, same distance.

The advance and retreat are then practiced with either foot foremost, after which the instructor commands.

Face to the Rear!

At the word "Rear," when either foot is foremost, the class face about, turning on both heels in the direction in which they are facing at the time, so that the front becomes the rear. For example, the right foot being foremost, face about to the left, and vice versa with the left foot foremost. The pupils remain in the same place, but reverse the position.

Rear—Leap!

At the word "Leap," spring from the ground with both feet, and leap to the rear, striking the heels together in the air, as in the rear leap in boxing, and come to the ground, with feet apart, at guard distance as before.

These preliminary exercises being thoroughly understood, the class is provided with staves as high as the head, and the intervals are extended to about eight feet, so as to allow the staves to be swung to the full extent of the arms without interference. No special costume is needed until actual staff play begins, when the pupils need hoods of stiff leather, padded inside, or, still better, broadsword masks, gloves padded at the knuckles, and leathern arm-guards. The instructor, seeing his class at the proper intervals, commands:

Attention!

Stand in position of soldier, facing the instructor, the staff perpendicular by the right shoulder, the end resting on the ground by the right foot, the right hand supporting it between the thumb and forefinger as in the dotted lines in the picture.

The instructor now commands:

For Staff Exercise—Ready!

The class raise the staves in their right hands, and catch them with the left, resting staff on front of thigh, as in the figure, right hand above the left both thumbs pointing same way.

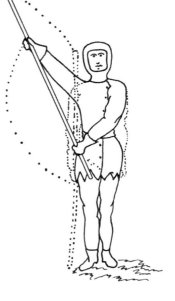

He next commands:

Left Shoulder—Staves!

Slide the right hand down the staff to the left, and throw the point over the left shoulder, as in the figure, throwing the right foot out to guard distance at the right, shoulders square to the front.

The instructor next commands:

Right Swing—One! Two! Three!

Throw the point of the staff up at the word "One," and swing a circle around the head, striking diagonally down on the right side, the staff returning to the shoulder.

At the word "Two," swing a second circle horizontally, the staff returning to the shoulder. At the word "Three," swing a third circle diagonally upwards, the staff returning to the shoulder as before.

The instructor next commands:

Right Shoulder—Staves!

The staves are brought over to rest on the right shoulder, in the same manner as they were on the left shoulder.

The instructor then commands:

Left Swing—One! Two! Three!

Executed in the same manner as from the left shoulder, and requiring no further explanation.

The class is then brought back to the position of "Ready," and instructor commands:

Change—Hands!

At the word "Hands," the position of each hand is altered, the staff inverted so that the thumbs point in the opposite direction to what they did at first, and the left hand becomes uppermost, the staff on the left hip. The exercise then proceeds in the following order, which explains itself:

Staff Swinging Exercise! Ready! Right shoulder staves! Left swing— One! Two! Front change! Left shoulder staves! Right Swing— One! Two! Face to the rear! Left Swing—One! Two! Face to the rear! Right swing—One! Two! Double advance! Right swing— One! Two! Rear leap! Right swing—One! two!

The exercise is thus repeated and varied till the pupils swing in any direction, either with feet and shoulder square to the front, or with either foot forward. Those exercises give the user of the quarter-staff the same ease and suppleness which the moulinets give with single-handed cane or single stick, and terminate the first lesson. The swings are made from the shoulder on account of the weight of the weapon which cannot be handled by the arms alone without unnecessary strain. This exercise will be found useful in handling heavy canes of *lignum vitæ*, which cannot be conveniently used with one hand. The figure below gives a sufficient idea of the general principles of staff-swinging.

XV.

THE USE *of the* STAFF

(continued).

The class in staff exercise having been practiced in swinging complete circles to either hand till they have acquired a complete mastery of the staff, are drawn up at open order and at a Ready, the right hand uppermost. The instructor then commands:

Right Guard!

Slide the right hand down to the left on the staff, throw the left foot to the rear, and the point of the staff over to the front, left hand above staff pointing diagonally forward and to the right. This constitutes a guard against the first blow, and the instructor then explains the different positions of the staff, from the left hand guard, just as in the cane exercise, the directions of blows and guards being the same (see Chapter XIII). The instructor next commands, successively:

Ready! Change Hands! Left Guard!

At the word "Guard" throw back the right foot, wheeling on left heel, and throw the staff down diagonally to the front, as in the figure. The instructor then shows the positions of the staff in right hand guards against the various blows, as in the previous exercise, and then practices the class in coming to either guard with either foot foremost, by the following commands:

Ready! Left Guard! Front Change! Right Guard! Front Change! Left Guard! Front Change! Etc.

All which requires but little explanation. In Left Guard the left foot is foremost; in Right Guard the right foot. Being on guard with either foot forward, a front change compels the hands to be changed, to secure the requisite inclination of the staff, and keep the proper hand uppermost.

The instructor, having fully perfected the class in changing hand and foot, so as to guard on any side, teaches next the thrusting guards, as follows: Being at right hand guard, left foot forward, he commands:

Thrusting Guard!

Slide the left hand down the staff to the middle, as in the figure, and throw up the staff, receiving the blow between the hands. This is the best guard to be adopted by a man of inferior strength, against an adversary who tries to beat down his guard by main weight of blow.

The guards being now thoroughly learned, the blows are taught, as in staff-swinging, by the commands:

Ready! Left Guard! Left Shoulder Staves! Right and Left Extend and Swing! One! Two! Three! Four! Front Change! Right and Left Extend and Swing! One! Two! Three! Four!

These blows will explain themselves, being the same as in single-stick or cane exercise, which has been given. The fifth blow is seldom used, as it is easily guarded and ineffective. With every blow the pupil extends to double distance, and returns to guard distance. The blows and guards are combined into an exercise as follows: The pupils are divided into pairs, and named "Front" and "Rear Rank" respectively. Front rank extends and strikes first blow; rear rank guards it, and then executes front change, extend and strike first blow, as in the figure, which represents the blow from right-hand guard.

The exercise then proceeds, with either foot forward (as shown in the first illustration below), by the following commands, which explain themselves as executed by each rank.

Parry and Return—First Blow! Second Blow! Third Blow! Fourth Blow! Etc.

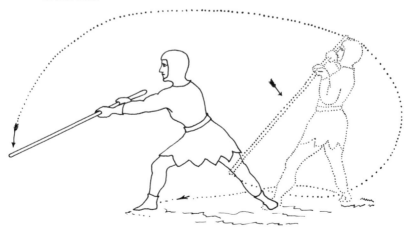

The use of thrusting guard is then taught (as shown in the final illustration) by the following exercise:

Thrusting Guard! Parry and thrust—First Blow! Second Blow! Etc.

The other blows are parried and returned in the same way, and need no further explanation.

The thrust may be used as a feint, the hands slid down the staff, ending the front change and extension with a blow. Sir Walter Scott describes this use of thrusting guard and thrust in his memorable description of the quarterstaff fight between Gurth and Much, the Miller, in the novel of "Ivanhoe."

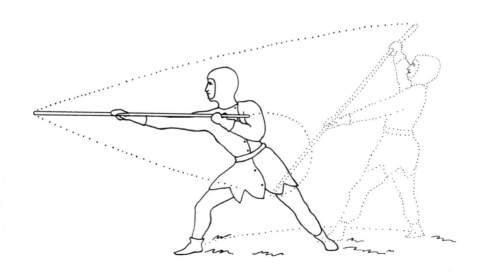

Monstery's Maxims

HERE ENDS the self-defense portion of Colonel Monstery's treatise on physical education. To close, it seems fitting to quote a few of his maxims:

"Be civil to all, and never seek a quarrel, but if one is forced on you, strike quick and surprise your opponent."

"Every gentleman should be able to protect himself from insult and violence, with or without weapons."

"Never consider yourself unarmed even if confronted by an armed man, for almost anything can be made into a weapon if properly used."

"He who lives by the sword, lives long."

"Follow nature in your living. Don't eat too much, but eat enough. Avoid dieting, and exercise in the open air when you can."

"The man of superior mind always makes the best fencer in the end."

"Above all things, never lose your presence of mind."

Monstery's Rules for Contests of Sparring and Fencing.

"An assault of arms should be conducted with the same precaution as if life itself was at stake."

— Colonel Thomas Monstery, *Turf, Field, and Farm*,
January 29, 1875

On Dec. 28, 1878, *The Spirit of the Times* published the New York Athletic Club's "Laws of Athletics," specifying the various rules and conditions under which contests of sparring, fencing, and wrestling were to be conducted. Two days later, Monstery responded, submitting his own commentary on the sections dealing with sparring and fencing. It included criticisms, suggestions, and additions, and was published in the next week's issue of *The Spirit of the Times*.

Following is Monstery's submission to the *Spirit*. For context, the New York Athletic Club's "Laws of Athletics" have been inserted where appropriate.

619 Sixth Avenue, New York City, Dec. 30, 1878.

Dear Spirit:

Observing the invitation by the New York Athletic Club published in last week's *Spirit*, for suggestions as to alterations and amendments of their laws of athletics, I beg leave to submit the following on those branches in which I may be said to have acquired some experience during my career of thirty years as a master of all arms. I offer these suggestions because the arts to which I refer are but little known and less practiced in the United States, and my object in offering them is to promote fair play, and to prevent as far as possible all sorts of sharp practice and unfairness. Dishonest advantages are too apt to be taken in contests of all sorts, and the object of nine-tenths of all athletic rules is to prevent them. I wish to comment on Laws 25, 26, 27, and 28 of the proposed code. They relate in their order, as above stated, to Sparring, Foil Fencing, Broadsword, and Singlestick. I will mention these in their order.

I. SPARRING:

NEW YORK ATHLETIC CLUB LAWS:

"(1.) Competitors shall spar in a space of 24 ft. square, or other suitable space, in socks, slippers, or shoes, without spikes. (2.) One attendant allowed outside the inner ring to each competitor. (3.) There shall be three rounds both in the trial and final bouts, and each round shall last three minutes. (4.) No wrestling, roughing, or struggling at the ropes. (5.) Time between each round, thirty seconds. (6.) Style in sparring is essential. The division of weight shall be: Feather, 115 lbs. and under; light, 135 lbs. and under; middle, 158 lbs. and under; heavy, over 158 lbs."

MONSTERY'S RESPONSE:

Rules 1, 2, 3, 4, and 5 are good as they stand, and require no special comment. Rule 6, however, is decidedly ambiguous, and, without further explanation, will open the door to any amount of unfairness. At present it reads: "Style in sparring is essential." This rule means anything or nothing, as the judge may decide, its interpretation solely on his opinion. This should not be. "Style," as understood by the rules, should be clearly defined. I suggest the following addition to the sentence as it stands: "Style shall be held to consist in striking and parrying in the same manner as in contests without gloves, where the hand is liable to injury from improper blows. Whipping, cutting and palming, and round blows will be considered bad style." The rest of Rule 6, defining heavy, middle, light, and feather weights, should be Rule 7, as it has now no connection with the matter placed before it in the same rule.

II. FENCING WITH THE FOIL
NEW YORK ATHLETIC CLUB LAWS:

"In fencing the following rules will be observed: (1.) The foil to be thirty-four inches long, have a flat blade, and be unattached to the hand or wrist by cord or string to prevent being disarmed. (2.) A free thrust must be followed by a pause, if this thrust has been successful. (3.) Reprisals or double thrusts being forbidden, the competitor who has lunged has to return on guard, to avoid hand-to-hand fight. (4.) Time or stopping thrusts, delivered without the lunge, count only in favor of the giver if not hit himself; if both are hit simultaneously, the count belongs to the competitor who has hit his opponent in the higher part of the body; if hit in the same line, the point is of no count. (5.) A disarm not to count for a point unless followed immediately by a thrust; if the foil is lost while making an attack and hitting the opponent, it is to count for one point. (6.) It is forbidden to parry or take your opponent's foil with the disengaged hand. (7.) If one of the competitors retire before the end of a play, he loses the play. (8.) The number of points to be not less than five nor more than ten, and to be decided by the judges or referee; the competitor first making the full number of points to win the play."

MONSTERY'S RESPONSE:

Rules 1, 2, and 3 require no special comment. The object of providing for a flat blade to the foil in Rule 1 is entirely to secure safety. The common cheap foils, usually sold in this country are square or nearly so, and if broken in a violent assault, as frequently happens, will inflict as bad a wound as a dueling sword. Their use has caused the death of more than one fencer by so-called "accident." Rule 4 should stop at the word "if not hit himself." The rest of the rule, providing that the count in simultaneous thrusts should belong to the party striking the upper part of the body is not only unwise, but directly calculated to encourage and protect the meanest sort of trickery and cheating. It is true that, at present, our amateur fencers, as a rule, fence fairly; but if this rule be persisted in, it is only a matter of time for them to become proficient in this sort of cheating, and to ruin the art of fencing in the United States for ever. There is only one safe practice to follow in foil fencing. This is to imitate as closely as possible the contest with the naked point. No one but a maniac would take thrust for thrust from an adversary with sharp points, unless, indeed, he were a very inferior swordsman, who wished to take some sort of revenge by piercing his enemy's shoulder, at the price of a mortal wound through his own lungs. By striking off this vicious provision, ample room will be left for the legitimate time-thrust and stopping-thrust, which are marks of the highest skill in fencing if the giver not be hit while delivering them. Rule 5 should read: "A disarm counts one point." As it stands, it puts a penalty on the skillful fencer, unless he performs the mean action of striking an unarmed adversary; and the second part of the rule goes without saying. The other rules need no further remark.

III. FENCING WITH THE BROADSWORD

NEW YORK ATHLETIC CLUB LAWS:

"In broad sword the following rules will be observed: (1.) The sword must be 34 in. long, have a flat blade, three-quarters of an inch broad at hilt and half-an-inch at point and be unattached to the hand or wrist. (2.) All cuts must be made with the edge of the blade upon any unprotected part of the body above the waist; no cuts with the flat of the blade allowed. (3.) A cut must be followed by a pause, if the cut has been successful. (4.) If both contestants are hit simultaneously, the count belongs to the competitor who has hit his opponent in the higher part of the body; if hit on the same line, there shall be no count. (5.) A disarm not to count for a point unless followed immediately by a cut; if the sword is lost while making an attack and hitting the opponent, it is to count for one point. (6.) Neither of the competitors must in any case allow his hands to come in violent contact with his opponent's body. (7.) The number of points to be not less than five nor more than ten, and to be decided by the judges or referee; the competitor first making the full number of points to win the play."

MONSTERY'S RESPONSE:

Rules 1, 2, and 3, are proper. Rule 4 is even worse than Rule 4 in fencing [with the foil], as the consequences of simultaneous blows with sabres cannot fail to be disastrous to both parties. In an actual sabre duel, their delivery would require two maniacs instead of one. The rule should read: "Where two cuts are delivered at the same time, the count belongs to the party who is extended. If both are extended, neither counts." Rule 5 is open to exactly the same objection as Rule 5 in fencing, and should be read the same as I have suggested. I see no reason why Rule 7 of fencing should not be inserted in the law for broadsword, and the same remark applies to the next law, relating to singlestick.

IV. FENCING WITH THE SINGLESTICK

NEW YORK ATHLETIC CLUB LAWS:

"In single stick the following rules will be observed: (1.) The stick must be unattached to the hand or wrist, and may be any ordinary walking cane, that shall be agreed upon by the contestants; if they fail to agree, the referee shall decide. (2.) Blows only count on the mask and arms. (3.) A blow must be followed by a pause, if the blow has been successful. (4.) If both contestants are hit simultaneously, the count belongs to the competitor who has hit his opponent on the higher part of the body; if hit on the same line there shall be no count. (5.) A disarm not to count for a point unless followed immediately by a blow; if the stick is lost while making an attack and hitting the opponent, it is to count for one point. (6.) If one competitor seizes his opponent's stick with his hand (his own weapon being free), it shall count one point. (7.) Neither of the competitors must in any case allow his hands to come in violent contact with his opponent's body. (8.) The number of points to be not less than five, nor more than ten, and to be decided by the judges and referee; the competitor first making the full number of points to win the play."

MONSTERY'S RESPONSE:

Rules 4 and 5 of this exercise are open to the same objections as the corresponding rules in fencing and broadsword, and for exactly the same reasons. Rule 7 of fencing should certainly be inserted in singlestick.

I would here remark that the name "singlestick" for the exercise described in the law, should be changed to that of "walking-stick," "cane-play," or "cudgel-play." The English singlestick is only employed as a cheap substitute for the sabre or broadsword in practice, and cuts on the body and limbs are therein properly counted. In cane-play, on the other hand, blows are very properly counted on the head or arm, as such would be the only really disabling blows that could be delivered with a walking-stick or cudgel. In practicing cane-play, these vulnerable points being protected by a helmet or mask, and a gauntlet, the players receive no injury.

One last remark on fencing, and I have done. I earnestly recommend the following additional rule in foil contest: "Rule—. The buttons of the foils must be chalked between each round, and the competitors must wear a black body cover, to show the mark of a clean thrust, and distinguish the same from a glance." This rule, if adopted, will prevent a great deal of cheating—cheating which is sure to ensue if tournament-at-arms become popular in the United States. At present this cheating is confined to the lowest class of European professionals. Let us not, through ignorance, admit it into the society of American gentlemen amateurs.

Yours,
Thomas H. Monstery
Champion at Arms of North and South America

Glossary

Below is a list of terms which appear in Colonel Monstery's treatise. It should be noted that Monstery does not define all of his terms, but assumes some knowledge on the part of the reader. Therefore, some definitions in this glossary have been taken from other texts of the period: for boxing, they have largely been excerpted from L. Hillebrand, *Sparring: Or, The Theory and Practice of the Art of Self Defence* (Philadelphia: Fisher & Brothers, 1864); for fencing, they have been taken from Alfred Hutton, *Fixed Bayonets* (London: Clowes & Sons, 1890). Except where specifically noted, the definitions that appear in quotation marks are Monstery's.

Boxing, Kicking, and Grappling

Advance—"The pupil doubles the distance between the feet by stepping forward with the left foot, and follows with the right." (Ch. 2)

Back-Fall—A grappling technique that is used to throw the adversary on his back. (Ch. 9)

Butt—A strike executed with the head. (Ch. 10, 11)

Certain Time—Strikes executed "when your [antagonist] expects it" are executed in "certain time." (Ch. 10)

Chancery—To get an adversary "in chancery" is to get him in a headlock or choke. (Ch. 9)

Counter Parries—See Effective or Counter Parries.

Cutting—"A malicious way of striking," effective only when used with gloves, "as it forces aside the padding of the glove, and the blow comes with the edge of the hand, made harder by one fold of leather." (Ch. 10)

Double Advance—"The pupil makes two quick steps forward with the left foot, following with the right, being especially careful not to diminish the distance between the feet from that presented at Guard." (Ch. 2)

Double Retreat—"The pupil steps back quickly twice with the right foot, following with the left, as in the advance, and preserving same distance between the feet." (Ch. 2)

Effective or Counter Parries—Parries "which, besides warding off the antagonist's blow, expose him to your own blow in a position where he finds it difficult to parry." (Ch. 7)

Evasion—Moving "out of the line of an enemy's blow... faster than the blow can be sent," while at the same time coming "within striking distance of the opponent without danger to yourself." (Ch. 8)

Feint—A strike made from out of distance, intended to draw a reaction from the antagonist. (Ch. 4)

Front Change—An action "executed by stepping to the front with the right foot from position of 'Guard,' wheeling on the left heel. This brings the right foot foremost, and the position of the arms should be reversed accordingly." (Ch. 9)

Front Head-Lock—"It consists in catching [the antagonist] round the neck, and clutching his head under your arm, catching his outside wrist if possible, then punching away at his face." (Ch. 9)

Full-arm blow—A strike made from the wrist resting on the hip, diagonally upward to the antagonist's (or dummy's) face with either hand. Monstery notes that blows in an actual set-to are not delivered in this manner, but that "it is, however, necessary to learn them, in order to make the subsequent half arm blows really effective." (Ch. 2)

Guard—"This is the position best calculated for attack and defence, and is that which a sparrer assumes in front of an antagonist." (Hille-brand, 16)

Half-arm blow—A strike made from the elbow resting on the hip, or any position further forward. (Ch. 3)

High blow—A strike directed at the centre of the face of the antagonist. (Ch. 3)

Imperfect Parry—"Those parries where the arm is exposed to injury by meeting a blow with the side of the wrist at right angles to the coming shock." (Ch. 5)

Inside Leg Parry—A defense, using one's left leg, against the kick of an antagonist. (Ch. 11)

Leap—"Leap to the rear with both feet simultaneously, and in the leap strike the left heel smartly against the right, coming down with the feet apart at the distance of Boxing Position or Guard . . . it enables you to escape a blow that you cannot parry, and leaves you on guard against an enemy who must throw himself open to follow you." (Ch. 2)

Line of Attack—"The perpendicular line which passes through the centre of the antagonist's body . . . All blows must be delivered in this line or they lose their power and pass the enemy." (Ch. 3)

Line of Power—"The straight line from the [left] elbow along the back of the hand to the first knuckle of the middle finger." (Ch. 2) In an 1887 interview, Monstery defines the line of power as proceeding "from the shoulder to the knuckles of the second, third and forefingers." (Introduction)

Low blow—A strike directed at the "mark," or pit of the stomach, of the antagonist. (Ch. 3)

"The Mark"—"The pit of the stomach." (Ch. 2)

Outside Leg Parry—A defense, using one's right leg, against the kick of an antagonist. (Ch. 11)

Palming—A method of striking, effective only when used with gloves, described as "slapping with the open hand." (Ch. 10)

Parry—"Parrying is beating a blow out of its line, with the hand or arm, to make it miss the point aimed at." (Hillebrand, 16)

Perfect Parry—"Those [parries] which strike off a blow without exposing the delicate bones of the arm to injury. There are six simple parries, namely: Right and left, high and low, outside, and right and left high, inside." (Ch. 5)

Purring—A British style of fighting characterized by shin-kicking, sometimes (but not always) utilizing grappling holds, and typically practiced while wearing heavy clogs or iron-toed boots. (Ch. 11)

Rear Change—An action "executed by stepping to the rear with the left foot, wheeling on the right heel. It is used in defensive motions, and leaves the right foot out as in front change." (Ch. 9)

Rear Head-Lock—"If you lead, and your antagonist uses an evasion, so that you find your arm over his shoulder, throw it instantly back round his neck, throw the weight of your body on him, and then grasp your own wrist with the other hand, trying to lift him from the ground, his whole weight on his neck, squeezing with all your might, so as to strangle him." (Ch. 9)

Retreat—"The pupil doubles the distance between the feet by stepping back with the right, following with the left." (Ch. 2)

Return—"The Return Blow is one which is generally struck immediately after a parry." (Hillebrand, 16)

Rough-and-Tumble—A no-holds-barred, historical style of American fighting characterized by punching, kicking, grappling, hair-pulling, scratching, biting, and eye-gouging. (Ch. 11)

Round blows—"Nearly all blows which are not delivered in a somewhat straightforward line, and which are commonly used by unskilled persons, are called round blows. They generally take effect upon the sides of the body or head, either with the fist or open hand."

(Hillebrand, 87). Monstery simply states that these blows "are like cutting." (Ch. 10)

Savate—A form of French street fighting that developed in Paris and Marseilles during the nineteenth century. Also known as *Boxe Française*. (Ch. 11)

Set-To—"A Set-to is a sparring contest between two opponents, and is generally divided into short combats called rounds, with periods of rest between." (Hillebrand, 17)

Spar—"The correct definition of the word Boxing is striking with the fist. That of Sparring is the practice for improving the art. This term is also applied to those habitual motions of the arms during a contest, while watching an opportunity to strike." (Hillebrand, 17) Also, "To make the motions of attack and defense with the arms and closed fists; use the hands in or as if in boxing, either with or without boxing-gloves; practise boxing." (Whitney, 5795)

Stopping Blow—A strike "given so as to anticipate [the] opponent's blow," i.e., executed in the same time as the antagonist's attack. (Ch. 6) "The stop blow is simply delivering a blow at the time the opponent is about to land one, thus stopping the blow." (Fisher, 400)

Uncertain Time—Strikes executed "after feints, and when [the antagonist] does not expect it" are executed in "uncertain time." (Ch. 10)

Whipping—A method of striking, effective only when used with gloves, "executed with the end of the fingers after a blow has been parried, with a flirting motion of the wrist over the guard, so as to catch the opponent's face with the leather of the glove, and graze the skin." (Ch. 10)

FENCING:

Advance—"Double the distance between the feet . . . and then bring up the rear foot to 'Guard' distance." (Ch. 14)

Assault—"The exercise with blunt weapons, representing in every respect a combat with sharps, in which we execute at will all the maneuvers of the fencing lessons." (Hutton, 136)

Assault of Arms—"An exhibition of fencing with various weapons." (Hutton, 136)

Back Change—Wheel on the heel of the backmost foot while throwing the foremost foot back, so that the position of the feet are reversed, the interval between the feet remaining the same. (Ch. 14)

Change Hands—"The position of each hand [on the quarterstaff] is altered, the staff inverted so that the thumbs point in the opposite direction to what they did at first, and the left hand becomes uppermost, the staff on the left hip." (Ch. 14)

Espadoning—"An improvement on the moulinets, as it simulates the blows more closely. . . Espadoning is borrowed from the sword exercise, and is meant to simulate the blows exactly. It accustoms the pupil to keep his hand high in striking, and to end his blow with the point lower than the hand in all high cuts." (Ch. 13) The word "espadon" is taken from the obsolete French, and refers to a broadsword or saber. (Hutton, 143)

Extend—With the quarterstaff, "double the distance between the feet by advancing the forward foot." (Ch. 14)

Face to the Rear—"When either foot is foremost . . . face about, turning on both heels in the direction in which [one is] facing at the time, so that the front becomes the rear. For example, the right foot being foremost, face about to the left, and vice versa with the left foot foremost. The [fencer] remains in the same place, but reverses the position." (Ch. 14)

Feint—Feints are "simulated attacks made at various points in order to draw the parry, while the real attack is directed at the opening left by it." (Hutton, 143) Monstery merely notes that these are "blows... which are to draw the [adversary's] guards to a certain position..." (Ch. 13)

Front Change—Wheel on the heel of the foremost foot while throwing the backmost foot forward, so that the position of the feet are reversed, the interval between the feet remaining the same. (Ch. 14)

Guard—"That position of person and weapon which is the most ready for both attack and defence." (Hutton, 145)

Leap—"Spring from the ground with both feet, and leap to the rear, striking the heels together in the air, as in the rear leap in boxing, and come to the ground, with feet apart, at guard distance as before." (Ch. 14)

Moulinet—A circular cut with the broadsword or saber. Depending upon the type of weapon used and the style of fencing, moulinets could be executed from the wrist, elbow, or shoulder. Here, with the cane, Monstery instructs the reader to moulinet from the wrist, without bending the arm or elbow. (Ch. 13) "A series of exercises of circular cuts, taught in order to afford facility in the use of the sabre, &c." (Hutton, 148)

Parry—"The movement of the weapon which wards off or stops a thrust or a cut." (Hutton, 148)

Retreat—"Double the distance between the feet by stepping back with rear the foot, then drawing back the forward foot to 'Guard' distance." (Ch. 14)

Return—"A hit delivered immediately after having parried an attack." (Hutton, 150)

Swing—A circular, cutting motion made with the quarterstaff, executed from the shoulder. (Ch. 14)

Time-thrust—A hit "which is effected just as the opponent is meditating an attack, or when he comes forward with movements either too wide or too slow." (Hutton, 141, 153)

Bibliography

A New Book of Sports. Reprinted from the Saturday Review. London: R. Bentley and Son, 1885.

Baines, Edward. *The History, Directory, and Gazetteer, of the County Palatine of Lancaster.* Liverpoole: W. Wales & Co., 1821.

Bibb, Henry. *Narrative of the Life and Adventures of Henry Bibb, an American Slave.* New York: printed by author, 1850.

Bolster, Jeffrey. *Black Jacks: African American Seamen in the Age of Sail.* Cambridge, MA: Harvard University Press, 1997.

Canfield, H. S. "Monstery: Soldier of Fortune" in *Everybody's Magazine* 7, no. 4, October, 1902.

Chicago of Today: The Metropolis of the West. Chicago, Ill.: Acme Publishing and Engraving Co., 1891.

Encyclopædia Brittanica: A Dictionary of Arts, Sciences, Literature and General Information, vol. 11, Cambridge, MA: University Press, 1910.

Engelhardt, Fred. J. *The American Rowing Almanac and Oarsman's Pocket Companion.* New York: Fred. J. Engelhardt, 1874.

Fewtrell, Thomas. *Boxing Reviewed; or, the Science of Manual Defence.* London: Scatcherd and Whitaker, 1790.

Fisher, George, ed. *Physical Training, vol. 14.* New York: Physical Director's Society of the Y.M.C.A. of North America, 1906.

Fitz, George Wells. *American Physical Education Review, vol. 9.* Boston: American Physical Education Association, 1904.

Flinn, John J., ed. *The Handbook of Chicago Biography.* Chicago: The Standard Guide Company, 1893.

Fox, Richard Kyle. *Boxing: With Hints on the Art of Attack and Defense and How to Train for the Prize Ring.* New York: Richard K. Fox, 1889.

Gaugler, William. *The History of Fencing.* Bangor: Laureate Press, 1998.

Georgii, Augustus. *A Biographical Sketch of the Swedish Poet and Gymnasiarch Peter Henry Ling.* London: H. Bailliere, 1854.

Gorn, Elliot. "Gouge and Bite, Pull Hair and Scratch," *The American Historical Review* 90 (Feb. to Dec. 1985).

Gracián, Baltasar. *The Art of Worldly Wisdom.* New York: Barnes & Noble, 2008.

Heraud y Clavijo de Soria, D. Antonio. *Manual de Esgrima y Duelo.* Paris and Mexico: Libreria de la Vda de Ch. Bouret, 1912. Rpt. of 1892 edition.

Hillebrand, L. *Sparring: Or, The Theory and Practice of the Art of Self Defence.* Philadelphia: Fisher & Brothers, 1864.

Hutton, Alfred. *Fixed Bayonets: a Complete System of Fence for the British Magazine Rifle, Explaining the Use of Point, Edges, and Butt, Both in Offence and Defence; Comprising also a Glossary of English, French, and Italian Terms Common to the Art of Fencing, with a Bibliographical List of Works Affecting the Bayonet.* London: Clowes & Sons, 1890.

Johannsen, Albert. *The House of Beadle and Adams and its Dime and Nickel Novels, vol. 2.* Norman: University of Oklahoma Press, 1962.

Lemoine, A. *Traité d'éducation physique: Atlas par A. Lemoine, Lt Aide de Camp.* Gand: Lithographie de G. Jacmain, 1857.

Milligan, Robert. *The Fetish Folk of West Africa.* London: Fleming H. Revell Co., 1912.

Monstery, Col. Thomas H. *New Manual of the Art of Swimming, as Taught by the Monstery Method.* New York: *The Spirit of the Times,* 1878.

Nyblæus, Gustaf. *Fäktlära.* Stockholm: P. A. Norstedt & Soner, 1876.

Price, Edmund. *The Science of Self Defence. A Treatise on Sparring and Wrestling, Including Complete Instructions in Training and Physical Development. Also, Several Remarks Upon, and a Course Prescribed for the Reduction of Corpulency.* New York: Dick & Fitzgerald Publishers, 1867.

Riboni, Giuseppe. *Broadsword and Quarter-Staff Without a Master: Broadsword Fencing and Stick or Quarter-Staff Play, After the Latest European Practice Adopted in the Military Schools of France and Italy, and the United States.* Chicago: E. B. Myers, 1862.

Schenström, R. *Gymnastique médicale suédoise: Traitement des maladies chroniques, Méthode Ling.* Paris: 26, Avenue Friedland, 18[?].

Bibliography

Sinclair, Sir John. *The Code of Health and Longevity, Vol. II.* Edinburgh: Arch. Constable & Co., 1807.

Strömborg, N. *Gymnastiklära: efter P.H. Ling och G. Branting. Första häftet, Fäktlära.* Stockholm: F. E. Östlund, 1857.

Whitney, William Dwight, ed. *The Century Dictionary and Cyclopedia*, vol. 7. New York: The Century Co, 1897.

Whittaker, Capt. Frederick. *The Sword Prince: The Romantic Life of Colonel Monstery, American Champion-at-arms.* New York: M. J. Ivers & Co., 1884.

Wilson, Francis. *Francis Wilson's Life of Himself.* Cambridge, MA: Houghton Mifflin Company, 1924.

Wilson, Francis. *Recollections of a Player.* New York: De Vinne Press, 1897.

Woelmont, Baron Henry de. *Notices généalogiques: Quatrième série.* Paris, 1928.

Wright, Frank Lloyd. *Frank Lloyd Wright: An Autobiography.* New York: Duell, Sloan and Pearce, 1943.

NEWSPAPERS

The American Historical Review
Army and Navy Journal
Auburn Daily Bulletin
Boston Daily Globe
Brooklyn Daily Eagle
Cincinatti Daily Times
Chicago Tribune
Cleveland Leader
Cleveland Plain Dealer
Columbus Journal
Courrier des États-Unis
Critic-Record
The Current
Daily Alta California
Daily Graphic

Daily Inter Ocean
Daily Morning Call
Denver Post
Detroit Free Press
El Monitor Republicano
Everybody's Magazine
*Hampshire Telegraph
   and Sussex Chronicle*
Harper's Weekly
Los Angeles Herald
Macon Telegraph
Memphis Daily Avalanche
Mexican Herald
National Police Gazette
New York Clipper

New York Evening Telegram
New York Herald
New York Sun
New York Sunday Telegraph
New York Times
Omaha Daily Bee
Omaha World Herald
Pittsburgh Press
Sacramento Daily Union
San Francisco Bulletin
San Francisco Call

San Francisco Chronicle
The San Francisco Newsletter
The Spirit of the Times
St. Paul Daily Globe
Sunday Inter Ocean
Turf, Field, and Farm
Utica Saturday Globe
Victoria Daily Colonist
Weekly Inter Ocean
Washington Post
Western Medical Reporter

Monstery's Writings

The chapters of Monstery's *Physical Education for Gentlemen* appeared in the following corresponding issues of *The Spirit of the Times*:

Chapter 1: December 22, 1877
Chapter 2: December 29, 1877
Chapter 3: January 5, 1878
Chapter 4: January 12, 1878
Chapter 5: January 19, 1878
Chapter 6: January 26, 1878
Chapter 7: February 2, 1878
Chapter 8: February 9, 1878

Chapter 9: February 16, 1878
Chapter 10: February 23, 1878
Chapter 11: March 2, 1878
Chapter 12: March 9, 1878
Chapter 13: March 16, 1878
Chapter 14: March 23, 1878
Chapter 15: March 30, 1878
Appendix: January 4, 1879

Illustration Credits

Page ii: Photograph signed "Col. Thos. H. Monstery," to Leon Regnier, May 2, 1885. Courtesy of Hargrett Rare Book and Manuscript Library / University of Georgia Libraries.

Page 2: Francis Wilson, *Recollections of a Player* (New York: De Vinne Press, 1897), 26.

Page 5: Image from the editor's collection.

Page 7: Francis Wilson. *Recollections of a Player* (New York: De Vinne Press, 1897), 26.

Page 12: Edward Jump, *San Francisco at the Fair* (California: 1864). Courtesy of the Bancroft Library, University of California, Berkeley. BANC PIC 1963.002:0469—D. The key identifying Monstery in this image was published in *The San Francisco Newsletter*, July 20. 1916, 30.

Page 17: Francis Wilson, *Francis Wilson's Life of Himself* (Cambridge, Mass.: Houghton Mifflin Company, 1924), 46.

Page 23: *National Police Gazette*. November 2, 1895, 4.

Page 25: *National Police Gazette*. June 9, 1906, 2.

Page 27: "Maids of Muscle" in *Weekly Inter Ocean*, November 30, 1886, 5.

Page 30: Fred. J. Engelhardt, *The American Rowing Almanac and Oarsman's Pocket Companion* (New York: Fred. J. Engelhardt, 1874), 145.

Page 32: Francis Wilson, *Recollections of a Player* (New York: De Vinne Press, 1897), 26.

Page 40: *The Spirit of the Times*. December 29, 1877, and Richard Kyle Fox, *Boxing: With Hints on the Art of Attack and Defense and How to Train for the Prize Ring* (New York: Richard K. Fox, 1889), 6–7.

Page 57: *Chicago of Today: The Metropolis of the West* (Chicago, Ill.: Acme Publishing and Engraving Co., 1891), 181.

Page 64: Image from the editor's collection.

Page 66: Image from the editor's collection.

Page 74: *The Spirit of the Times*. December 29, 1877.

Page 77, left: *The Spirit of the Times.* December 29, 1877.

Page 77, right: *The Spirit of the Times.* December 29, 1877.

Page 78: *The Spirit of the Times.* December 29, 1877.

Page 82: *The Spirit of the Times.* January 5, 1878.

Page 83: *The Spirit of the Times.* January 5, 1878.

Page 92: *The Spirit of the Times.* January 19, 1878.

Page 93: *The Spirit of the Times.* January 19, 1878.

Page 94: *The Spirit of the Times.* January 19, 1878.

Page 95, left: *The Spirit of the Times.* January 19, 1878.

Page 95, right: *The Spirit of the Times.* January 19, 1878.

Page 97: *The Spirit of the Times.* January 26, 1878.

Page 102: *The Spirit of the Times.* February 2, 1878.

Page 103: *The Spirit of the Times.* February 2, 1878.

Page 104: *The Spirit of the Times.* February 2, 1878.

Page 114: Edmund Price, *The Science of Self Defence* (New York: Dick & Fitzgerald Publishers, 1867), 81–82.

Page 115: Edmund Price, *The Science of Self Defence* (New York: Dick & Fitzgerald Publishers, 1867), 83–84.

Page 127: *National Police Gazette.* November 25, 1899, 3.

Page 129: A. Lemoine, *Traité d'éducation physique: Atlas par A. Lemoine, Lt Aide de Camp.* (Gand: Lithographie de G. Jacmain, 1857), plate 15.

Page 130: *National Police Gazette.* June 14, 1890, 10.

Page 131: *National Police Gazette.* June 14, 1890, 10.

Page 134: *National Police Gazette.* February 22, 1879, 13.

Page 135: *Harper's Weekly*, New York, August 15, 1874.

Page 147: D. Antonio Heraud y Clavijo de Soria, *Manual de Esgrima y Duelo* (Paris and Mexico: Libreria de la Vda de Ch. Bouret, 1912), 167. Reprint of 1892 edition.

Page 150: *The Spirit of the Times.* March 16, 1878.

Page 152: *The Spirit of the Times.* March 16, 1878.

Page 154: *The Spirit of the Times.* March 16, 1878.

Page 155: *The Spirit of the Times.* March 16, 1878.

Illustration Credits

Page 158: *The Spirit of the Times.* March 16, 1878.

Page 168: *The Spirit of the Times.* March 23, 1878.

Page 170: *The Spirit of the Times.* March 23, 1878.

Page 171: *The Spirit of the Times.* March 30, 1878.

Page 172: *The Spirit of the Times.* March 30, 1878.

Page 173: *The Spirit of the Times.* March 30, 1878.

Page 174: *The Spirit of the Times.* March 30, 1878.

Page 175: From the editor's collection.

Page 176: John J. Flinn, ed., *The Handbook of Chicago Biography* (Chicago: The Standard Guide Company, 1893).

About the Author

THOMAS H. MONSTERY was born on April 21, 1824, in Copenhagen, Denmark. At age twelve he joined the Danish navy, and he later completed his military training at the Royal Military Institute of Gymnastics and Arms in Copenhagen. He went on to study at the Central Institute of Physical Culture in Stockholm, Sweden, from which he graduated a master of arms. As a soldier he fought under twelve flags in Europe and the Americas, took part in numerous revolutions, ascended to the rank of colonel, and participated in more than fifty duels with the sword, knife, and pistol. After immigrating to the United States, he embarked on a distinguished career as an instructor of fencing and pugilism, opening schools in Baltimore, San Francisco, New York, and Chicago, and became recognized as one of the finest fencing masters in America. He died on New Year's Eve, 1901.

About the Editor

BEN MILLER is an American filmmaker and author. He is a graduate of New York University's Tisch School of the Arts, was the winner of the Alfred P. Sloan Foundation Grant for screenwriting, and has worked for notable personages such as Martin Scorsese and Roger Corman. For the last ten years, Miller has studied fencing at the Martinez Academy of Arms, one of the last places in the world still teaching an authentic living tradition of classical fencing. He currently serves as the Academy's chef de salle and has authored articles for the Association of Historical Fencing, focusing on the fencing and dueling of the American colonial period.

About North Atlantic Books

North Atlantic Books (NAB) is a 501(c)(3) nonprofit publisher committed to a bold exploration of the relationships between mind, body, spirit, culture, and nature. Founded in 1974, NAB aims to nurture a holistic view of the arts, sciences, humanities, and healing. To make a donation or to learn more about our books, authors, events, and newsletter, please visit www.northatlanticbooks.com.